Excel at Graduate Interviews

Palgrave Career Skills

Excel at Graduate Interviews

How to Make the Best Impression with Recruiters

Bruce Woodcock

 macmillan education   palgrave

First published 2016 by
PALGRAVE

Palgrave in the UK is an imprint of Macmillan Publishers Limited, registered in England, company number 785998, of 4 Crinan Street, London, N1 9XW.

Palgrave Macmillan in the US is a division of St Martin's Press LLC, 175 Fifth Avenue, New York, NY 10010.

Palgrave is a global imprint of the above companies and is represented throughout the world.

Palgrave® and Macmillan® are registered trademarks in the United States, the United Kingdom, Europe and other countries.

ISBN 978–1–137–53584–9 paperback

This book is printed on paper suitable for recycling and made from fully managed and sustained forest sources. Logging, pulping and manufacturing processes are expected to conform to the environmental regulations of the country of origin.

A catalogue record for this book is available from the British Library.

A catalog record for this book is available from the Library of Congress.

Printed in China

To my wonderful wife and sons: Beth, Gavin and Ewan

Contents

Introduction

Contents

Who is this book for?

This book is aimed at university students looking for graduate jobs, students looking for placements and internships and also postgraduates and recent graduates. Graduate job changers will also find it valuable, as will graduate recruiters and careers staff in schools and universities. Although aimed at new graduates, much of the content will hold value throughout your working life.

How will it help you?

As a university careers adviser, I find that many students, despite being outwardly confident, are worried about finding a job after graduation, especially those studying non-vocational degrees. Because they are worried, they sometimes leave things until the last minute, hoping the problem will go away.

The graduate job market is demanding, and getting a graduate job requires careful research, planning and commitment. Many graduates don't identify their skills or relate these skills to the jobs they are interested in; they don't research jobs to sufficient depth and don't prepare enough for interview. Paradoxically, many employers are struggling to recruit graduates: there is a shortage of graduates with initiative and the right attitude. The ones who have these qualities stand out like diamonds, and all employers are actively searching for these.

Qualifications are important, but only as a starting point. Skills such as communication are another part of the equation, but what employers value most is the right attitude: determination in the face of adversity, coupled with creativity, adaptability, a desire to keep learning, a 'can do' attitude and willingness to take responsibility. Graduates with excellent academic records are frequently overtaken a few years into their careers by graduates with poorer degrees but the above qualities.

Many students fear interviews. They are afraid of the unknown as they don't know what questions will be thrown at them. In this book you'll find out how to answer many of the common questions that crop up in graduate interviews, plus strategies to deal with those you can't predict. Lack of confidence is a key reason people fail at interview, and you'll learn how to become more confident by demystifying the process.

This book is based on recent developments and research in graduate recruitment. It uses plain English, diagrams and interactive exercises, and is positive but realistic in approach. It encourages you not just to read but to take actions which will improve both your interview skills and many other aspects of your job hunting.

Why are interviews used?

The point of an interview is for the interviewer to see if you meet the requirements of the job. These include your personal qualities, how well you express yourself, and your motivation and enthusiasm. Recruiters have an idea of these from your application, but the interview assesses you in person. If you've got this far, it suggests that your application has persuaded the employer that you could fill the requirements and that you have something valuable to offer.

It's also your chance to meet somebody from the organization and assess him or her: are they offering what you want? Graduate interviewers are typically friendly. They will of course, ask you demanding questions which stretch you, but will also want to convince you that their organization is a great place to work. If an interviewer is unfriendly, you may decide that they are typical of their organization and that you don't wish to work in such a negative culture.

Companies spend thousands of pounds recruiting graduates, and this only includes the cost of advertising the vacancy, visiting universities to give presentations or to attend careers fairs, sifting online applications, paying for aptitude tests and using managers at interviews and assessment centres. The hidden costs are much higher. A typical graduate training scheme may last two years, in which, as well as paying your salary, the company also pays for training, professional development and examinations, mentoring and the cost of teaching you skills and the staff time taken up by this; these costs can easily reach six figures.

The graduate recruitment process

The following diagram shows the main stages of typical selection processes for graduates. At the top is the process for a large organization which recruits many graduates and has a number of stages, and underneath that is one for a smaller organization. Small companies can't usually afford complex online application procedures, and so selection may be based on just a CV and an interview. Large companies tend to start their recruitment much earlier, as they can predict their recruitment needs much further in advance.

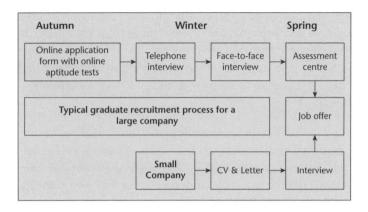

So it's important to get it right: the last thing an organization wants is to spend all this money and then get the wrong graduate or to have the new recruit leave after a year, so there is a lot of pressure on interviewers to choose the right person.

Content

The book begins with a chapter on preparing for interview: why this is vital and how to go about it. We then move on to how to make a good impression in the first few minutes of the interview, as many interviews are decided at this stage, and how to conquer those interview nerves, so you don't freeze right at the start.

Next we look at the different types of interview question and how to answer these, and then the most common type of question you are likely to face: competency questions and strategies for answering these. We also look at interviews for different roles and how telephone and Skype interviews differ from face-to-face interviews.

Finally, we look at the end of the interview and what to do afterwards, and you have a chance to put everything together by trying a practice interview.

The interview process

The following diagram neatly sums up the stages of a typical graduate interview process, and we'll be expanding on these stages as we go through the book.

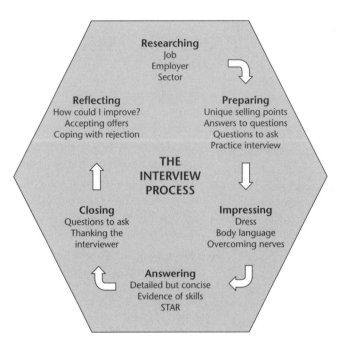

Researching
Job
Employer
Sector

Reflecting
How could I improve?
Accepting offers
Coping with rejection

Preparing
Unique selling points
Answers to questions
Questions to ask
Practice interview

THE INTERVIEW PROCESS

Closing
Questions to ask
Thanking the
interviewer

Impressing
Dress
Body language
Overcoming nerves

Answering
Detailed but concise
Evidence of skills
STAR

Preparing for the interview

Contents

What you will learn in this chapter

- How preparation makes the difference between success and failure
- How to research the job, organization and sector and how to predict interview questions from the job description
- What questions to ask at the end of the interview and why this is important
- How to identify your unique selling points
- How to manage your social media presence to provide a professional image

If you have been called for an interview, you are already halfway to your objective of getting a job offer. It shows that the employer is seriously interested in you and that your application is on the right lines. Employers only shortlist a handful of candidates, so you should congratulate yourself on getting this far.

Failure to prepare is to prepare to fail

You won't get far trying to sink an unsharpened axe into a tree trunk, nor will you be successful at interviews without careful preparation. There are no short cuts! To make a change in any part of your life, you must commit the time to do so. The most important factor determining success at interview is good preparation. Most interviews are lost before the interviewee even enters the room. An interview is a game where you know most of the rules and must play by them.

> *'Give me six hours to chop down a tree, and I will spend the first four sharpening the axe.'*
>
> Abraham Lincoln

Research, research, research!

> *One interviewee asked the interviewer,* 'By the way, what is the name of this company?'

Insight from a student

One graduate was invited to interview for an internal audit position with an accountancy firm. Although she had an A Level in mathematics, her degree was in English literature, and she didn't feel she would have much chance of success against the business graduates she would be competing against at interview. She felt her best strategy was to find out as much as possible from the Web about the firm, accountancy and particularly what internal audit involved.

A few days later she got a phone call offering her the job. At the interview she had been asked to explain what she knew about internal audit, and she had managed to talk at length about it. When she was offered the post, she was told that none of the other candidates had known much about internal audit. The interviewers had been impressed with her research, especially as it was unrelated to her degree.

An employer may spend up to £100,000 in recruiting a graduate, training the person and paying his or her salary for their first three years. Graduates are seen as the future management of organizations, the clean slate on which the company ethos can be imprinted. No organization will risk this amount of time and money on graduates who don't know what the job involves, whether they have the right attributes and if they will be comfortable with the training required, because these graduates might drop out if they find they aren't suitable. This is why the employer will look for evidence of careful research.

Employer story

One company director said that nine students had applied for a post he had on offer, but he had rejected every single one of them as not one had taken the trouble to take a detailed look at the company's website. When he asked, 'What does our company do?' and 'What are our main products?', none could give a coherent answer. He decided that all future applicants would be required to apply via the company website, so at least they would be forced to take some notice of it.

Research the job and organization

Most interview success comes from what can't be seen during the interview. Like an iceberg, it's the hidden part which has the most impact: the preparation you do beforehand.

The interview iceberg

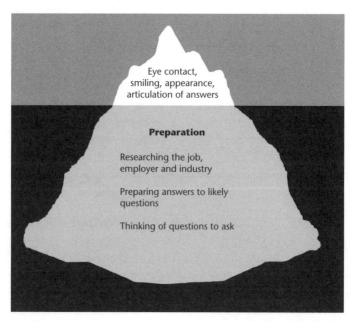

You must show an interest in the organization and the wider environment in which it operates as you will be asked about this. Teachers need to be aware of current educational trends, journalists must know of the developments in web journalism and social workers have to be aware of the latest government initiatives.

> *'I find that the harder I work, the more luck I seem to have.'*
>
> Thomas Jefferson

Carefully read the organization's website. Try to find out how many people work for the organization. Research its turnover and profits, share price and products or services. Find out who the organization's competitors are: you may be asked to name these and to say which ones you've applied to. Organizations are reassured if you are applying to their competitors – if you haven't applied to any, it suggests a lack of career focus.

Relate your own experience to the organization you are applying to. You may be working in a shop just to earn money, but this can give you an insight into business. What are the good and bad points about this employer? If you were a manager, how could you improve the company?

Tips from an employer

- Thoroughly research the company and the market that it's in. Find out who's interviewing you and his or her remit within the company, and then tailor your preparation for this audience.
- Thoroughly prepare for the usual competency-based questions. Ensure you have at least two to three good examples for each competency, and practise your answers out loud.
- Have some intelligent questions prepared to ask during (or at the end of) the interview.

Parvinder Matharu, Managing Director of Newton Recruitment

Employers will test your knowledge by asking questions like these:

- Why are you applying for this job?
- Why do you want to work for us?
- What do you know about our organization?
- What do you think the job you would be doing entails?
- What skills do you think are required to do this job?
- Why do you wish to enter this industry?
- What are our main products and services?
- What are the problems facing our company at this time?
- What changes have there been in the industry recently?
- Where do you see yourself in five years' time?
- What skills did you gain from your work experience?

One interviewee recited the history of the company from its beginning but got several facts completely wrong.

Use Glassdoor, The JobCrowd and other websites to find out about the experiences of other students who've had interviews. Just enter 'Interview feedback for... company'. If it's a large organization, you may find lots of feedback, including the questions asked and any tests or group exercises given.

Tips from Rebecca, a biology graduate

Prepare thoroughly – as the application form was not very long, the interviewer picked up on every little thing I'd written, so make sure you know your form well and can expand on the points you made. She began by asking me to tell her about myself and what I'd done, and this actually took up much of the interview. Always make sure you do research on the company on why you want to join them, as this is usually one of the first questions. Show eagerness and enthusiasm when you answer questions. Keep smiling, even when you are under pressure – show that you can handle it. You'll certainly be nervous, but once the interview starts, it just flows by. The emphasis is on getting to know the real you, rather than just ticking boxes.

Rebecca, applying for accountancy role

Analyse the job description and person specification

To persuade the interviewer that you are the right candidate, you have to understand the employer's needs, to see things from the company's perspective and to gather the evidence to prove your case. The best way to do this is to analyse the **job description** and the **person specification**.

The job description

Job descriptions are written statements of the duties, responsibilities, working conditions, qualifications, knowledge and skills required to perform effectively in a specific job. They are based on a job analysis in which the tasks, knowledge and skills needed for the role are examined.

Exercise: Detecting interview questions from the job description

As a customer support analyst, you provide customers with phone and face-to-face support and resolve queries.

The role involves
- providing first-line support to customers and staff;
- participating in the training of new staff; and
- ensuring smooth implementation of processes.

You must be someone who
- enjoys working in a team;
- can work to tight deadlines;
- has initiative/flexibility to react to changing circumstances;
- has strong organizational skills;
- has strong customer service skills;
- has strong communication skills, both written and verbal;
- has excellent problem-solving abilities;
- has good time management skills: can handle multiple tasks; and
- is proficient in Microsoft Office, including Excel and Word.

Highlight key words above which describe the main activities and skills required
If you were the interviewer, what questions might you ask based on the skills and activities you've highlighted? Write these down.

A student's story

A few years ago a health authority interviewed eight graduates for their management training scheme, but only one of these was put forward to the final assessment centre. The student selected had an average academic record and, although pleasant, didn't seem to have any attributes that the other candidates didn't also possess. At the end of the day, I asked the interviewer why this person had been selected. She said it was quite simple. He had, on his own initiative, arranged and spent a day at a hospital shadowing a senior manager, finding out as much as he could about what the job involved. His knowledge of the Health Service, how it worked and the skills required was far better than that of any of the other candidates she had seen, and his initiative and motivation had greatly impressed her.

The person specification

The person specification indicates the employer's needs and is usually included within the job description. Person specifications are used in large organizations with big HR departments such as multinational companies and public sector employers: local authorities, hospitals, universities and the Civil Service. They are normally shorter than the job description, and you probably won't get a person specification if the company is small.

If you are sent a person specification, the interview will be structured around it. It is commonly divided into essential and desirable characteristics. Study it carefully and think of evidence you could provide to show you meet these characteristics.

The interviewer will have a form with all the criteria listed and a list of questions based on these criteria. Each interviewee will be asked the same questions, and answers will be scored depending on how well they fit the criteria. This is called a competency-based interview (see Chapter 4, 'How to STAR at competency questions').

Exercise: Relating the person specification with what you have to offer

Experience and Knowledge	Essential	Desirable
Experience of prioritizing competing demands	✓	
Experience of working in a customer service environment		✓
Knowledge of Microsoft Office	✓	
Skills and Abilities		
Able to achieve targets within agreed time scales	✓	
Able to work autonomously and in a team	✓	
Numerate, with excellent IT skills		✓
Ability to adapt to changing priorities	✓	

Look at the specification and write down questions that the interviewer might ask you. Think of examples to show how you've gained relevant experience. Are there any areas where you might be weak?

Prepare questions to ask the interviewer

At the end of the interview you'll normally be asked if you have any questions. The interview is a two-way process, and you are selecting the organization just as much as they are selecting you. The interview is a conversation which you are partly in control of, and asking questions will help you appear to be an assertive, confident candidate. You are in a position of power, as the employer is relying on you to provide the information needed.

An interview is a two-way process

You don't necessarily have to wait until the end of the interview to ask questions. Sometimes the opportunity to ask a question arises naturally in the course of the interview, and if so, take it.

I have known occasions where the interviewer has suddenly switched from asking the candidate questions to telling the candidate how good the company is compared to its competitors. This may mean that they've identified you as an outstanding candidate who is likely to get offers from competitor companies, and so they are trying to secure you.

> *One interviewee asked,* 'Would it be a problem if I'm angry most of the time?' *Perhaps not, if you wish to work as a debt collector!*

Sensible interviewers treat interviews as a meeting of equals. They treat all interviewees with respect and aren't overly formal or serious. They sell their company to the interviewee by setting a positive example of the company culture. If this is good, people want to work for the company. These interviewers will get many applicants and easily retain staff. Interviewers who practise old-fashioned stress interviews put candidates on the defensive and turn off the most talented candidates, who will join friendlier organizations.

Why must you ask questions?

This is your chance to find out more about the job and the company so you have the information to decide whether to accept the job. If you don't ask questions, the interviewer may suspect that you lack interest in the job; you lack curiosity, initiative or self-confidence; or that you just haven't done any research. Not asking questions or asking poor questions may be sufficient reason for the interviewer to fail you.

> *Another interviewee asked,* 'Do I have to dress for the next interview?' *I think she meant 'dress smartly'!*

If you really feel that the interviewer has answered all of your questions, you could say that you've carried out careful research and that all of your questions have been answered by the company website, but it still sounds weak: 'I was going to ask about the training I'd get, but you've answered all the questions I prepared.'

You could ask the interviewer about his or her own experience of working for the organization, as this can't have been answered beforehand and people like talking about themselves. You can also use this time to mention anything important that hasn't come up in the interview. Or, 'Is there anything else you would like to know about me?' or, 'I'd like to say that now I've found out more, I'm really interested in this job.'

Think of the questions you wish to ask well before the interview. The interview isn't a memory test: it's fine to write down the questions you wish to ask, but don't write them in a large notebook you have to rummage in your bag to find. Instead write them on a piece of card that will fit in your pocket. Have a number of questions written down, even if you only intend to ask a couple, as some of your questions might be answered in the interview.

Tips from an employer

It has been said that interviewers only ask the question 'Do you have any questions?' because it would be impolite not to, after grilling you with questions for the last 40 minutes, but we disagree. Even if that were true and until that point your interview had not gone as well as you would have liked, this is your one chance to potentially change the course and success of your interview by turning it on its head.

Can you imagine yourself in an interview for the job you really want, competing against many others? If you are the only one who has prepared a written list of questions that don't just relate to what is already on the website, what is the crucial message you are sending out? *I want this job and I've worked for this. I am organized, well informed, interested in your company, and I come prepared for my meetings.*

Be cautious, though. Interviews normally have a set time allocated. If you were to try to ask all of these questions, your interviewer would become agitated and cut the meeting short.

Grovelands Recruitment

What questions should you ask?

Good questions are on training and career development; bad ones are those answered by the employer's website or ones on salary, holidays, perks, flexible hours and pensions, as these suggest that you are only interested in the job because of the benefits. If the salary hasn't been specified, it's okay to ask about this, but you must ask other questions as well. Questions that show evidence of careful research are also good: *'I see that last year you opened a new factory; how is this affecting your production?'*

The best questions are those that you really want to know the answer to. If you really do want the job, these should be easy to formulate based on your research and will show you have a good insight into the job and organization. Make sure you've researched the employer carefully so that you are not asking about things you would be expected to know.

Questions not to ask

Don't ask questions just for the sake of it. Here are some embarrassing questions asked by interviewees:

- What is it that you people do in this company?
- Why aren't you in a more interesting business?
- Would the company be willing to lower my pay?
- What is your zodiac sign?
- Will you pay to relocate my horse?
- Does your health insurance cover pets?
- Do you have a policy regarding concealed weapons?
- I know this is off the subject, but will you marry me?
- Why am I here?

How many questions should you ask?

Interviewers only have limited time available for you to ask questions at the end of the interview, so don't outstay your welcome by asking too many; you are the interviewee, not the interviewer. Asking too many questions can annoy the interviewer if he or she is behind schedule and other interviewees are waiting. If you know that your interview should end at 3 p.m. and it's already after that time, only ask one or two questions. Watch the interviewer for signs of encouragement or impatience; if the interviewer is gently snoring, then perhaps you've asked one question too many!

Two or three questions are about right for a graduate job. The more senior the post, the more questions you would be expected to ask. If you are offered the job, you can always ask more questions at this point.

Some questions you could ask the interviewer

- Please tell me about your training programme?
- What support would I get for professional development?
- How does the company promote personal development?
- Where would I be located?
- How often would my performance be appraised, and what criteria would you use to measure performance?
- What are the duties and responsibilities?
- What would be the main priorities in my first year?
- What kind of career paths have other graduates taken?
- How do you see this role developing?
- What is the turnover of graduates?
- How much say would I have in setting my targets?
- How much discretion would there be for me to make my own decisions?
- When would I be given responsibility?
- Will there be travel involved?
- Would there be opportunities for using my language skills?
- How would you describe the working atmosphere?
- What is your personal experience of working for this organization?
- How would you see the company developing in future?
- What are the long-term objectives of the organization?
- How much do people socialize together outside of work?
- What is the corporate culture, the way of doing things?
- Have you any reservations about my application and if so what are these?
- How is the economic climate affecting your business?
- What are the biggest challenges affecting the organization at the moment?

Identify your unique selling points (USPs)

Your unique selling points (or USPs for short) are strengths you convey during the interview to make you stand out from other interviewees. These could be an excellent academic record, evidence of key skills required in the job or relevant work experience. They are the attributes that make you an attractive applicant.

You are marketing yourself to the employer in the same way you would sell a car. You would emphasize its good points and play down the bad ones. You would not advertise it as 'Four wheels and an engine'; instead, you would say, 'One careful owner, low mileage and a new set of tyres.'

Use every opportunity in the interview to put across your USPs. If the interviewer asks you questions such as 'What are your strengths?', 'Why should we take you rather than other candidates?', 'How would your best friend describe you?' or 'Tell me about yourself?', or at the end of the interview asks you, 'Is there anything we haven't covered?', it's an ideal opportunity to mention your USPs.

Listing your USPs will boost your confidence. After all, if you can't convince yourself you can do the job, you won't convince the interviewer.

Some example USPs

- Getting a First in your exams (academic study)
- A high mark for a group project (teamwork and organizing skills)
- Duke of Edinburgh Award (determination)
- Captaining a sports team (leadership)
- Raising £300 for charity (community involvement)
- A summer job in a shop where you developed strong communication skills

- Working in a part-time job while studying (time management)
- Starring in a school play (coping with pressure)
- Language skills or ability to work across cultures (multicultural awareness)
- Travelling to the United States on your own to work as a summer camp counsellor (independence)

One way to get your USPs across is called the **elevator pitch**. Imagine you were in an elevator with the managing director and you had just the 30 seconds' ride to the top to sell yourself to her, how would you do this? For example,

> I'm Vivian Choi a final-year student studying history at the University of York. I achieved 67 per cent in my exams last year and have a strong interest in marketing, having done several modules and a project on this. I have extensive experience of customer service in which I found myself good at negotiating with and persuading customers. During my degree, I successfully combined my studies with work and other commitments, showing myself to be self-motivated and well organized. I show pride in all the work I do, work well under pressure and love a challenge. I have a drive to see things through to completion, and I try to learn something new from every experience because I believe there is always room for self-improvement.

Preparing your elevator pitch can be useful at the start of the interview if the interviewer asks you to talk about yourself, but it can also be used to introduce yourself in a professional manner at careers fairs, employer presentations and similar circumstances.

Exercise: Write your own elevator pitch

Think back through your life and focus on times when you've done things you are proud of, where you've learned a lot or developed relevant skills. Make a list of these points you would like to get across during an interview.

When you've written your pitch, practise it on a friend or family member to get feedback.

Check your social media presence before interview

For many students, the Internet is their main way of finding a job and a well-developed online presence through blogging, social media and networking can demonstrate that you have the desired skills and knowledge. It's especially important for business communications careers such as marketing, advertising, PR and the media. Social media is now an important communication platform, and many employers now use it to check candidates for suitability, particularly via LinkedIn.

> *Facebook is like a fridge. You know there is nothing new inside, but you check it every 10 minutes.*

You must manage your online presence and pay attention to privacy settings on your social media accounts. Google yourself to see if anything inappropriate comes up and also what is positive about you. Employers have rejected candidates because of what they found online, so protect your online reputation. Take ownership of your Web presence by limiting who can post to your profile and by monitoring posts in which you've been tagged. Think twice before you post: if you wouldn't want your parents to see it, then don't put it on your social media.

By developing your personal brand, you can accomplish the following:

- Increase your employability
- Establish a strong, professional social media presence
- Display your proactive nature
- Get noticed by potential employers
- Develop important relationships
- Protect your online privacy

LinkedIn is a business-orientated social networking site with 15 million users in the United Kingdom, and students are the fastest growing group. It is the top social media site for job-hunting so it's well worth putting your professional profile on LinkedIn (this is basically a cut-down CV without personal details such as address and age). Make sure your page sells you and mentions your career goals. It provides opportunities to network online with professionals; there are groups for different regions and also institutions such as universities. Put a professional photo in your profile, as people are four times more likely to connect to you if they can see your picture.

> *One interviewee was asked,* 'Do you post about work on Facebook?'

Many employers use **Facebook** to promote their brand and graduate programmes and to allow candidates to network with graduates and recruitment staff. You can pick up useful tips on the company and their recruitment processes that help you appear well informed. Set your Facebook privacy to high, so pictures of drunken nights out aren't visible, and make sure that your profile picture looks professional. Smile a little in your picture: research[1] found that people with positive expressions such as upturned eyebrows or a smile, are more likely to be seen as trustworthy.

Twitter can follow companies, brands and issues. Recruiters make much use of Twitter, dispersing information about their organizations and posting vacancies. You don't have to tweet yourself: you can just follow companies, brands, people or issues of interest; get a feel for current issues; and retweet their tweets. You can use your own tweets to show your interest in a career by tweeting about current issues in the sector you wish to work in. Your Twitter bio should include your degree and some relevant skills – all in 140 characters.

Writing a blog can show your writing skills and knowledge of a particular field, and other sites such as YouTube (for video CVs), Google+ and Viadeo can be useful.

Be wary of identity theft

When posting to your social media sites or replying to a job advert, if you have any doubts about the validity of the organization, be careful about what information you give. The following are not needed by employers and could lead to identity theft, so don't include them:

- Date of birth. Because of equal opportunity legislation, you don't have to disclose your age on a CV, but if you wish to do so, just give your year of birth.

- Place of birth
- Marital status
- Copies of birth certificate/passport or bank details

Compile your pre-interview checklist

A few days before your interview

❏ Carefully research the career area, job sector and employer.

❏ If there is a job description and person specification, read these carefully as questions are often based on these. Prepare examples of how your skills match those listed.

❏ Reread your CV or application form (which you've kept a copy of) from the perspective of the interviewer, and try to anticipate questions he or she might ask. Think about any problems the interviewer may focus on and how you could deal with these. Put yourself in the interviewer's shoes and think of what you would want to ask.

❏ Prepare answers to the obvious questions, such as *'Why do you want this job?'* You can probably anticipate 80 per cent of the questions you will be asked with careful research and by using sites such as Glassdoor. Don't learn your answers by heart as you'd sound stilted in the interview, but do write down in bullet points the key points in your answers. This will help you to memorize them so your responses become automatic. Practise speaking your answers out loud to see how they sound.

❏ Prepare questions to ask, and write these down on a small piece of card to take with you.

❏ Check the location of the interview, and print off maps.

❏ Plan your route carefully, leaving plenty of spare time in case of traffic jams or delayed trains.

❏ Check train times and buy rail tickets.

❏ Get your hair cut.

❏ Choose your outfit and iron it.

❏ If you have a disability which may make the interview harder for you, tell the employer so appropriate adjustments can be made.

❏ Carefully research the job, employer and sector.

❏ Read your application form or CV again with a highlighter pen, and identify questions that might be asked.

❏ If you know the name of your interviewer, check his or her profile on LinkedIn.
❏ Make sure that your social media presence doesn't show you in a bad light.
❏ Try a practice interview with a friend.
❏ Don't take qualifications, awards and other records of achievement. Certificates are only asked for when an offer of employment has been made. For creative jobs, such as graphic design, architecture and journalism, interviewers may want to see a portfolio of your work.

The evening before

❏ Put your list of USPs and questions to ask in your pocket.
❏ Pack a copy of your CV/application form to refer to before the interview and a copy of your CV for the interviewer if it might be needed.
❏ Charge your phone, and enter the number of the employer so you can ring for directions or inform the interviewer of delays.
❏ Take a pen and notepad, money for a taxi, handkerchief and perhaps a small bottle of water, but not unnecessary clutter.
❏ Take a smart briefcase or bag if needed, but not your battered old rucksack.
❏ Check travel times again.
❏ Exercise releases endorphins and relieves stress, helping you to sleep, but coffee or alcohol may hinder sleep.
❏ Don't spend too long doing last-minute revision – better to relax and have a clear head.
❏ Set your alarm and get an early night.

On the day of the interview

❏ Eating breakfast will increase your energy levels.
❏ Don't drink lots of liquid: you don't want to need the toilet during the interview.
❏ Check the weather forecast, and take a coat and umbrella if necessary.
❏ Check for any train delays or traffic problems on your route.

Finding out more

On the Web

- **Glassdoor** www.glassdoor.co.uk – excellent website with interview processes and questions for many companies
- **TheJobCrowd** www.thejobcrowd.com – interview tips for lots of organizations.

Reference

1   E Hehman, JF Ale and J Freeman, 'Static and dynamic facial cues differentially affect the consistency of social evaluations' (2015, August), *Personality and Social Psychology Bulletin*, 41(8), 1123–34.

Further reading

S Rook, *The Graduate Career Guidebook: Advice for Students and Graduates on Careers Options, Jobs, Volunteering, Applications, Interviews and Self-employment* (Palgrave Study Skills, Palgrave, 2013).

First impressions

Contents

What you will learn in this chapter

- How first impressions are vital in setting the tone for the interview
- How to get your body language right
- How to conquer those inevitable nerves and ways of boosting your confidence so you shine

When you arrive

If you go by car, you have the advantage of being able to wait in it if you arrive early. If the weather is fine, you may like to walk around the area: exercise will help to keep nerves at bay.

Aim to arrive at the location about 15 minutes before your interview. Being late for an interview is inexcusable and will probably lead to rejection. If you can't arrive on time for an interview, how can you be trusted to be on time for important meetings? Also, when you arrive, you will probably have to report to reception and be given instructions for where to go for your interview. If it's a big building, it may take some time to get there. The reason some people are always late for appointments is that they greatly underestimate the time they need to get

How not to plan your journey

One candidate went to an interview in Lincoln, near the cathedral, and on checking the map estimated it was just a short walk from the railway station. She found, however, that she had misjudged the scale of the map, and the walk was also up a very steep hill. She arrived completely out of breath, but fortunately just in time for the interview.

ready. Have a time frame for every task. Getting there a little early will allow you to become comfortable with your surroundings. This will decrease your stress levels and allow you to relax so that you are in a positive frame of mind. Don't arrive more than 20 minutes early as this runs the risk of making you more nervous if you have to wait too long. Also, busy staff may feel that they have to talk to you, perhaps annoying them by taking them away from their work.

Icebreaker questions

Often the first question the interviewer asks at the start of the interview, or even before, whilst taking you to the interview office is 'How was your journey?' The interviewer isn't assessing your answer; it's just an icebreaker to help you relax, as you must know the answer. If your journey was difficult, don't make it sound too bad, or this could make you sound like a moaner – be brief, friendly and cheerful. Don't give a very short answer such as 'Okay' as it's an opportunity to show you can make small talk, and it will also help the interviewer to relax. Similar questions follow:

- It's a nice day today, isn't it?
- You're studying history, aren't you?
- Are you enjoying university life?

Be friendly to everyone

The first person you meet will probably be a receptionist who will be expecting your arrival. Be polite and friendly to and appreciative of him or her and everyone else you meet as they may well be asked for their impression of you. Look around the waiting room for features such as prizes the organization has won, professional magazines about the field of work, products they make or folders with press cuttings about the organization. Switch off your mobile phone at this point – a ringing or vibrating phone during the interview will not impress!

Two US researchers[1] followed 100 students trying to get their first job. They analysed these students' CVs for qualifications and work experience and talked to the interviewers afterwards. Surprisingly, the main factor in deciding which ones were selected was whether the candidate appeared to be a pleasant individual. The successful interviewees:

- Smiled and made a lot of eye contact.
- Showed a genuine interest in the interviewer and gave genuine compliments.
- Praised the company, so find something you genuinely like about the organization.
- Asked interesting questions, for example, 'What is your personal experience of working for this company?'
- Talked about subjects unrelated to job, but that interested the candidate and interviewer.

Sometimes an interview will start with an overview of the company and the role you are being interviewed for. It's also quite common for interviewees to be given a tour round the workplace perhaps as part of a group. Show an interest in what you are seeing, and ask some questions about what is done in particular departments and what it's like working there.

What to wear

The way you dress for interview demonstrates your professionalism. Taking care over your appearance can be as important for interview success as your qualifications. You need to convey an image of reliability, trustworthiness and attention to detail. Wearing casual clothes suggests you don't take your career seriously and shows a lack of commitment, whereas if you know you look right, you don't need to worry about how you look and can simply focus on making a good impression. You are showing how well you will represent the company's brand by the clothes you wear.

> *One girl bought some very smart, three inch heels for her interview. Being nervous and not used to her new shoes, she twisted her ankle whilst teetering along just before the interview: so make sure that whatever you wear is comfortable as well as smart.*

Invest in a smart dark suit, plain and classic in style.[2] Most organizations lag behind the latest fashions, so err towards the conservative. It tends to be easier for women as women's suits may be suitable for both formal and smart casual situations. Keep things simple and classy. Neutral colours are safest. Navy blue, black or grey suits or jackets and a contrasting soft white, cream or pale blue shirt or blouse work well. Odd patches of bright colour, such as a classy but simple tie, can add to your impact, but keep these minimal and in stylish classical colours such as burgundy or blue. A plain, neutral look suggests a professional outlook. Also don't wear so much aftershave or perfume that the interviewer has to open the window to prevent asphyxiation. In one recent study, women being assessed by other women for management posts were regarded as less employable if they wore a skirt above the knee and unbuttoned an extra button on their blouses.[3]

Don't take clutter with you, as it will detract from your image you wish to present of being well organized and efficient. It may also make you more flustered: take a single smart briefcase, bag or handbag if you need one at all. If you are female take a briefcase and put the essentials from your handbag in this.

> *Dress the part! Another interviewee thought I already looked like a teacher as I dressed in a full skirt suit. It makes you feel confident and gives a good impression.*

What is business casual dress?

One student had an interview with a major financial services firm and was asked to wear smart casual dress. He rang them up to find out what they meant by this and was told it was about the same as smart interview dress but without the tie!

If asked to dress business casual, men should wear a jacket or blazer, an open-necked shirt (with collar) or in summer perhaps a smart polo shirt with cords, chinos or cotton trousers with a belt and smart shoes. Women should wear smart trousers or a skirt, with a shirt or smart top. Your cleavage should be covered, and wear smart shoes.

Is the suit dead?

Many young professionals now believe the age of the suit is over, with business casual dress replacing it. They feel what they wear has no influence on their productivity at work. In recent years men's fashion has become less formal, with open-collar shirts now the norm. More companies have adopted a business casual dress code unless they are meeting with clients or have an important conference. This is especially so in the creative, fashion, media and technology industries with few employees, at companies such as Google, now wearing a tie and dress is business casual, but clothing is still more traditional in industries such as finance or law.

Even if being interviewed for a 'creative' role, you should dress as smartly as you can. Even if your day-to-day working clothes will be informal, taking the trouble to dress smartly at interview shows you really want the job. It also shows that you understand how to behave in a professional environment and would act appropriately if called upon to meet an important client.

If you do plan to dress informally for interview, make certain that this is acceptable. Check the company website for images of staff to see how they dress. Only wear casual clothes if the organization has informed you that casual dress is fine for the interview, and if in any doubt, err on the side of caution. Don't be like the interviewee who wore a T-shirt with 'Take this job and shove it' on the front.

Smart interview dress

Neat hair

Only one (plain) earring per ear. No nose rings or visible body piercing

✓ Minimal and un-obtrusive jewellery

✗ Jingling brace-lets, dangling earrings

Don't overdo the makeup or perfume!

✓ White or light-coloured plain blouse

✗ Low necklines, lots of frills

✓ Dark-coloured suit

✗ Big shoulder pads

No rings except a wedding or engagement ring

✓ Smart knee-length skirt with tights, or trousers

✗ Bare legs or very short skirt

✓ Dark, polished shoes

✗ Very high heels

The first few minutes

The first minutes of an interview are crucial. Many interviews are decided in the first minutes, with the rest of the interview involving checking that this first judgement is correct. So what can you do to survive those first minutes?

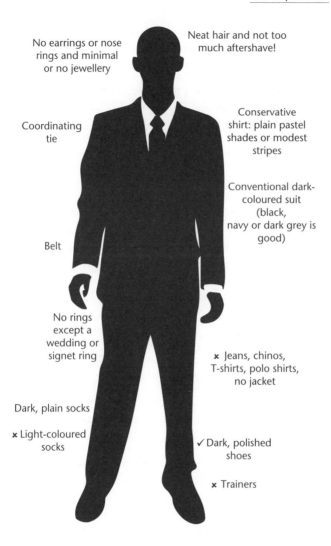

No earrings or nose rings and minimal or no jewellery

Neat hair and not too much aftershave!

Conservative shirt: plain pastel shades or modest stripes

Coordinating tie

Conventional dark-coloured suit (black, navy or dark grey is good)

Belt

No rings except a wedding or signet ring

✗ Jeans, chinos, T-shirts, polo shirts, no jacket

Dark, plain socks

✗ Light-coloured socks

✓ Dark, polished shoes

✗ Trainers

> *One candidate drank a large bottle of fizzy drink before the interview and spent the whole interview burping.*

Take several slow, deep breaths before you enter the room as it will help you to relax. Slow down and try to be really calm. Walk in tall with your chest out and shoulders back: you don't want to appear insignificant.

Knock before you enter, if the door is closed. Smile and look at the interviewer. If there is more than one interviewer, greet each one in turn, saying something like 'Hello, Ms Jones. I'm pleased to meet you'.

Shake hands firmly. Don't give the proverbial weak, 'wet fish' handshake, which suggests a lack of drive, but don't grip the interviewer's hand so firmly that you hurt them! Let the interviewer initiate the handshake, or you might be perceived as overconfident. A study at the University of Iowa found that  employers rated students with a firm handshake as more employable and as more likely to be offered jobs.[4] A firm handshake is perceived to show sociability, friendliness and dominance and sets a positive tone for the rest of the encounter, whereas weak handshakes suggest introversion and timidity. If there is more than one interviewer, be prepared to shake hands with each one. You also usually shake hands at the end of the interview.

Don't stand too close. The minimum acceptable personal space in Western cultures is about 40 cm unless you happen to be close friends, and invading this space will make the interviewer feel uncomfortable.

Wait to be invited to take a seat; it's impolite to sit down before this. Ask if you can take a seat if the interviewer forgets to ask you to sit down.

Read the room. If the interviewer is in a big chair behind a large desk, the interview may be traditional and formal, whereas if there is a small desk or none and the chairs are not far apart, it may be less formal: this arrangement also allows the interviewer to better observe your body language. Having said this, it could be that it was the only room available. Analyse the interviewer: is his or her body language open and positive or closed and unwelcoming? Does the interviewer look cheerful? Or weary after a long day?

The interview will normally start with a brief introduction and some small talk to help you to relax. Don't be afraid to initiate the conversation with light comments about the weather or your journey, such as 'It's a lovely day, isn't it?' This shows confidence without being pushy and breaks the ice. Also engage in light chat when being escorted to the interview room.

> *One interviewee dunked a biscuit into his tea and dropped it into his cup with a splash!*

Keep things simple. If offered tea or coffee, it's wise to decline as it makes one less thing that could go wrong: you may in your nervousness end up spilling it over your smart suit or wondering where to put your cup when you've finished it. Don't drink too much coffee before the interview either, as the mix of adrenaline and caffeine can be potent.

Tips from an employer

- Feel happy and positive as you walk into the interview.
- Visualize yourself sitting at the other side of the table, and then think, 'Which skills and attributes can I bring to the job that would add significant value in the short term and long term?' Aim to get your points across at the appropriate stages throughout the interview.
- Be ready to discuss *any* item on the job description and your CV.
- Don't interrupt the interviewer; listen and ensure you have answered the specific question.
- Body language is an important part of your communication. Get the basics right: for example ensure your handshake isn't floppy or too firm; maintain appropriate eye contact (without staring); don't slouch or fidget; sit confidently and try to mirror subtle shifts in posture without making it obvious; smile; and use your hands to positively gesture support for what you're saying.

Parvinder Matharu, managing director, Newton Recruitment

Boosting your confidence

Even the most confident of students can feel daunted by the prospect of an interview, so it's a good idea to remind yourself of your strengths, so you go into the interview in a positive frame of mind. Try this in the following exercise.

Self-assessment: What you have to offer

Choose five strengths (or more if you are especially talented) that most apply to you in the Wordle below. Feel free to add other strengths. For each strength you've chosen, note down an example of something you have achieved, you are proud of, or where you've received compliments.

Creative
Agile Persuasive
Likeable Resourceful Cheerful
Helpful Intelligent Inventive
Conscientious Practical Generous
Mature Charming
Adaptable Trustworthy Enterprising
Strong Honest
Determined Gentle
Resilient Polite
Patient Sincere
Warm

Humorous Optimistic Cooperative Independent Caring Dependable Versatile Careful

Strength	Where you have demonstrated this
1.	
2.	
3.	
4.	
5.	

Ask a friend what he or she thinks you are good at, and see how your friend's list matches yours. Each day, before your interview, read out your list of strengths and examples one or more times to remind yourself of what you do well. They should help you to feel more confident about yourself, and you may be able to use these examples at interview.

Body language

Many articles on interviews quote research by Mehrabian stating that interviewers are influenced mainly by body language (55 per cent), tone of voice (38 per cent) and only 7 per cent by the words spoken, but this was based on a speaker listening to a single word. Mehrabian dissociated himself from these interpretations.[5] Having said this, your body language does play a key part in interviews: we gather more information through our eyes than from any other sense.

The eyes

Maintain good eye contact during the interview: don't look down at your shoes, no matter how carefully you have polished them! People who look directly at us are perceived as more likeable and more attractive, and this is especially so if they are smiling. However, don't stare at the interviewer all of the time as this signals aggression.

How eye contact changes during interviews

We make more eye contact when we listen than when we speak, so look at the interviewer when he or she is speaking. The person who is speaking breaks eye contact more often, so it's fine to glance away sometimes when you are speaking, but when the person who is speaking changes, you should make eye contact. Glancing down suggests submission, whereas glancing to the side suggests confidence, so glance sideways rather than down.

	Interviewer asks question. Interviewee makes eye contact. Interviewer looks away some of the time.	Person speaking changes. Interviewer and interviewee both look at each other.	Interviewee replies. Interviewee looks away some of the time. Interviewer makes eye contact.
Interviewee	👀	👀	👀
Interviewer	👀	👀	👀

Smile!

Smiling is key to most successful interviews. We find people who look directly at us more likeable and more attractive, and this is especially so if they are smiling. Smiling while you are talking improves the way you look and sound and has a positive effect on your mood (see 'Fake it to make it' later in this chapter). When you frown, your body releases the stress hormone cortisol, whereas smiling reduces your stress level and also the stress level of the person you are smiling at. Don't, however, grin throughout the interview, or, like the Cheshire Cat's grin, your chances of success will rapidly disappear!

Speech

People tend to talk more quickly when nervous, and the pitch of their voice goes up. Speaking clearly and not too quickly helps, as a deeper, calm voice suggests authority, thoughtfulness and maturity, whereas an excitable and high-pitched voice suggests nervousness. Make an effort to slow down your speech if you notice yourself talking too quickly. See Chapter 7, 'Telephone, Skype and video interviews' for more about this.

Mirroring

People tend to prefer people who are similar to them, who have a similar voice, appearance and ways of behaving. Many interviewers would rather hire a candidate who may not have all the right skills, but who they like. Subtly mimicking facial expressions can make the interviewer feel more positive towards you. Strangers often carefully avoid mirroring each other's postures. Personal chemistry is very important during interview, and wise candidates focus on building rapport with the interviewer.

Mirroring the interviewer's posture can show empathy and agreement and helps you better understand the emotions the interviewer is feeling. If the interviewer is sitting upright, then it might be wise for you to sit upright too; if your interviewer is very relaxed, then you can be more relaxed in your posture. If the interviewer speaks very slowly, then you should perhaps slow down a little too. Wait a second or so before mirroring: HR managers are trained in body language and will notice such behaviours, so mirroring must be subtle. It can badly backfire on you if it is interpreted as mockery.

A personal example

When I'm interviewing students and there is a good rapport, it is fascinating to see the student subconsciously mirroring my behaviour: when I touch my chin, the student immediately does the same and isn't aware of doing this. I sometimes find that I am also subconsciously matching the student's body language: when the student changes posture, shortly afterwards I do the same.

Paraphrasing what the other person is saying to you and matching his or her tone and pace of speech is a verbal version of mirroring, and shows that you are listening carefully.

Other body language

Nodding your head slowly to show agreement shows interest and signals the interviewer to continue, but beware of nodding your head rapidly, which suggests impatience and overeagerness. If you've answered a question at length, watch the body language of the interviewer for signs such as head nodding or saying, 'Yes' or 'Uhmm', which indicate he or she wants you to continue.

Crossing your arms and legs can be taken as a sign that you are disinterested or defensive, so keep an open posture. Sometimes when I'm interviewing and we touch upon a sensitive subject such as poor exam results, I notice that students will cross their arms defensively. Unbuttoning your jacket when you sit down will also signify openness – that you have nothing to hide.

Leaning forward slightly in your chair suggests enthusiasm. Tilting your head slightly as you listen tells the interviewer that he or she has your complete attention. Rest your hands in your lap or on the arms of your chair if it has these. Clenching your fists also suggests tension, so keep your palms open.

Don't fidget! When you are nervous you may twirl strands of your hair, constantly stroke your chin or wring your hands without being aware that you are doing this. Keep your hands together in your lap.

How to conquer those interview nerves

Most students worry about interviews: they may have only had interviews for routine jobs such as shop work. The demanding job market adds pressure for you to perform well, so here are tips to help conquer those inevitable nerves.

You are expected to be nervous

Interviewers don't mind if you're a little nervous as it suggests that you really want the job, but they will expect your nerves to diminish after a few minutes. Everybody gets nervous in interviews, and the other candidates will be just as nervous as you are. Nerves don't show as much as we think: you always feel more nervous than you actually look. We know that we have butterflies in our stomach, but the interviewer probably won't realize this: we think people notice our behaviours much more than they really do. Understanding this should help you feel calmer.

Preparation is key

Fear of an interview is largely fear of the unknown: you don't know what you might be asked. 'What if they ask me a question I can't answer?' The more preparation you do, the more confident you will feel, so read Chapter 1, 'Preparing for the interview'.

The employer is seriously interested in you

You are an impressive candidate who meets the company's requirements or you wouldn't have been invited for interview.

Be yourself

Prepare carefully, but once you've done this, take the attitude that if you can't get the job by being yourself (albeit your best self), then the job may not be right for you. This doesn't mean that you don't make an effort, but once you get into the interview room, you should try to act naturally and not put on airs and graces. There is much evidence that the more genuinely and honestly you act, the more likeable you are perceived to be, and this genuineness has a bigger impact on your chance of success than coming across as overconfident.

It's not *that* important

It won't be the end of the world if you don't get this particular job. There will be other and perhaps better opportunities in the future.

Dress smartly

Dress smartly but comfortably. If you look good, you'll feel good.

Start the interview in a positive manner

Do this and it is likely to continue in this way. Smile, shake hands firmly and make good eye contact to get things off to a flying start.

The interviewer may be just as nervous as you!

Many managers are untrained in interview skills or only get a day's training before having to interview candidates. Managers may get drafted into interviewing to cover for an ill colleague or one who has an urgent meeting. So hold their hand and tell them not to worry! More seriously, a warm smile can help to put you both at ease, and if the interviewer isn't allowing you to sell yourself effectively, take any opportunity to talk about your USPs, as mentioned in Chapter 1, 'Preparing for the interview'.

Don't worry about the occasional mistake

Nearly everyone answers one question poorly, and it simply shows that you're human: very few interviewees give good answers to every question. If you flunk a question, just breathe deeply to calm yourself down, forget about it and prepare for the next question. Interviewers can be suspicious of candidates who appear faultless, feeling as if they haven't really got to know the candidate, who might be hiding weaknesses they can't discover. Interviewers may prefer candidates who have the odd foible, as these candidates come across as more genuine; even better if the candidate has sufficient self-awareness to know these weaknesses and has worked out ways to ameliorate them.

Think positive!

Writing down your worries before an interview helps to eliminate them from your mind, so they don't affect your performance on the day. So in advance of your interview try writing down everything that you are worried about.

> *Your mind is a garden,*
> *Your thoughts are the seeds.*
> *You can grow flowers,*
> *Or you can grow weeds.*
>
> William Wordsworth

Be careful how you talk to yourself as you are listening! Negative thoughts cause your body to release stress hormones which make you feel tense, so controlling your reactions becomes difficult. Conversely, thinking positive thoughts can slow your heart rate so you feel more relaxed. Disrupt the thought process and you remove the stimulus that causes your nervousness. Instead, make your adrenaline work for you: a job interview is an opportunity rather than a threat, and just like an athlete, you can channel this adrenaline to boost your positive energy and improve performance.

You do this by replacing negative thoughts with positive ones by a process known as reframing, a technique used in cognitive behavioural therapy (CBT). If you hear yourself thinking, 'I'm hopeless at interviews', then say instead, 'I've prepared well so I'll perform well'. If you think; 'I always get nervous', say instead, 'I'll be more confident this time as I have more knowledge than previously'. Cut down on words such as *always, never, worst* and *hate*. If you hear your inner critic, repeat instead your positive statements. Avoid asking 'What if …?' as this just generates worry. Instead take action on things that you can do something about. Most of the things you worry about never happen, and even if they do, you'll deal with them.

> *'As a single footstep will not make a path on the earth, so a single thought will not make a pathway in the mind. To make a deep physical path, we walk again and again. To make a deep mental path, we must think over and over the kind of thoughts we wish to dominate our lives.'*
>
> Henry David Thoreau

The process is simple, but like exercise, takes practice as you are creating a new habit. Each day, regularly stop and evaluate what you're thinking. If you find that your thoughts are mainly negative, put a positive spin on them.

Turning negative self-talk into positive

Below are examples of negative self-talk and how you could apply a positive spin to these.

Negative self-talk	Positive spin
I've never had a real interview before.	It will be a new and valuable experience.
I won't get this job.	I'm now really well prepared.
I'm hopeless at interviews.	I now know how to improve my performance.
Other candidates have more experience.	Potential is more important than experience for graduate jobs.
What if I make a mistake?	I don't have to be perfect.
I'm never going to manage my nerves.	Practice makes perfect!
I hate interviews.	They can be a great learning experience.
I won't improve.	The more I work at it, the more I'll learn.
I can't do it.	Yes I can! (to paraphrase Obama)
I talk too much/too little.	I'll practise interviews with friends.
I failed the interview.	But I now know where I'm going wrong.
Write here two things that you fear about interviews.	**Now put a positive spin on these fears, as in the examples above.**

Mindfulness

> *If you are unhappy, you are living in the past.*
> *If you are anxious, you are living in the future.*
> *If you are at peace, you are living in the present.*
>
> Lao Tzu

Mindfulness techniques can reduce stress in interviews and increase your focus and also your decision-making abilities. Organizations from banks and advertising agencies to schools and hospitals, government departments and charities now offer courses in mindfulness for staff. Google now has a mindfulness training manager, and the most popular of Google's training programmes is its mindfulness course which 2000 Google employees have undertaken.

Mindfulness simply involves switching off the non-stop chatter in your head as you jump from one negative thought to another. It allows you to regain control of your thoughts and behaviours, reducing the clutter in your mind, and brings your mind to a sharp focus. It allows you to see the world with fresh eyes by focusing on being in the present moment and finding happiness in the simple experiences of life.

The simplest mindfulness exercise can be done anywhere at any time. Simply focus on your breath for a minute or two. Breathe in and out deeply and slowly, holding your breath for a count of five once you've inhaled. Then breathe out slowly and effortlessly and repeat. Your thoughts will wander, but simply notice these thoughts without trying to control them or passing judgement on them, and return to watching your breath. This will release calming endorphins into your bloodstream, and you should soon feel relaxed. If you focus on your breathing as described for just 10 minutes a day, you will rapidly begin to calm and clear your mind, becoming more aware and more able to appreciate the present moment. Mindfulness practice can create measurable changes in under two hours. See the end of this chapter if you wish to learn more.

Visualization

Many top athletes use visualization techniques to help them prepare for major competitions, and studies have shown that sportspeople who used visualization improved their performance by up to 30 per cent.

Positive visualization embeds positive thoughts which produce positive behaviours.

In the days before your interview, visualize yourself going through the whole interview, step by step, and imagine everything going well: you confidently enter the room and shake the interviewer's hand; you answer all the questions really well; the interviewer is impressed; and you get the job.

Visualization exercise

Think of the times in your life when you were most happy.

What you were doing then that made these times so good?

Write these below.

Think of the times in your life when you were doing really well and performing successfully. Write these below.

Thinking about the things in life you are grateful for improves your mood and greatly reduces the stress hormone cortisol in your body. It also improves your energy and well-being. Write below three things you are grateful for: these might be family, friends, where you live or something you own.

Every day before your interview, read the above notes out to yourself when you need confidence.

Fake it to make it

Research by Amy Cuddy at Harvard Business School[6] found that adopting power poses such as standing up tall and stretching out for two minutes before interview led candidates to be evaluated more favourably and increased chances of a job offer by 20 per cent. Power postures such as standing with legs apart and hands on hips, as in the pictures of King Henry VIII and Superman, increase testosterone and decrease stress, making you feel more in control and more confident. Strike a power pose beforehand in the washroom, but don't try it in the interview itself or you will get some very strange looks. You can present a more imposing posture in interviews by sitting more upright and putting your shoulders back rather than slouching, which makes your body appear smaller.

Hands clasped behind your head can suggest arrogance or overconfidence, whereas steepling your hands with fingertips pointing upwards and touching each other can convey thoughtfulness and authority. Interestingly, standing with your hands on hips and legs apart is considered aggressive in Asian countries.

Taking this further, a technique called priming suggests having role models of people you aspire to be like. Choose people you admire, and watch documentaries about them or read their biography (for example Nelson Mandela's *Long Walk to Freedom*). Try to emulate their behaviour, and think how they would act in situations such as interviews.

Power music

Powerful music such as 'We Are the Champions' or 'Solsbury Hill' can also make you feel more powerful and in control, according to a recent study,[7] and cheerful music, such as Pharrell Williams's 'Happy', can put us into a more positive mood, so listen to your favourite cheerful and empowering songs on the way to your interview.

Checklist

❏ Arrive 15 minutes before the interview.
❏ Be friendly to everyone you meet.
❏ Dress smartly.
❏ The first few minutes are vital. Make eye contact with the interviewer, smile and give a firm handshake.
❏ Boost your confidence by reminding yourself of your good points.
❏ Get your body language right: don't cross your arms and legs, don't fidget, and consider 'mirroring' the interviewer.
❏ Nerves are expected at the start of an interview but can be minimized by careful preparation. Realize that the odd mistake won't prove fatal.

Finding out more

On the Web

● **Cognitive Behavioural Therapy and Mindfulness** GET Self Help www.getselfhelp.co.uk
● **Visualization techniques** Real Simple www.realsimple.com/health/mind-mood/emotional-health/visualization-techniques
● **First Impressions Count** http://ltss.beds.ac.uk/careers/first_impressions. Video by the University of Bedfordshire to help students with the first stages of interview preparation: how to dress, voice training, body language and confidence-boosting exercises
● **Quiz on body language in interviews** University of Kent www.kent.ac.uk/careers/interviews/nvc.htm

On the companion website (www.palgravecareerskills.com)

● Graphics showing power poses and other non-verbal communication in interviews

References

1   CA Higgins and TA Judge, 'The Effect of Applicant Influence Tactics on Recruiter Perceptions of Fit and Hiring Recommendations: A Field Study' (August 2004), *Journal of Applied Psychology*, 89(4), 622–32.

2 N Howlett, K Pine, I Orakçıoğlu and B Fletcher, 'The Influence of Clothing on First Impressions' (2013), *Journal of Fashion Marketing and Management: An International Journal*, 17(1): 38–48.

3 N Howlett, KJ Pine, N Cahill, I Orakçıoğlu and B Fletcher, 'Unbuttoned: The Interaction between Provocativeness of Female Work Attire and Occupational Status' (2015), *Sex Roles*, 72(3–4), 105–16.

4 GL Stewart, SL Dustin, MR Barrick and TC Darnold, 'Exploring the Handshake in Employment Interviews' (2008), *Journal of Applied Psychology*, 93: 1139–46.

5 Mehrabian misinterpretations https://en.wikipedia.org/wiki/Albert_Mehrabian – Misinterpretation.

6 A Cuddy, CA Wilmuth, AJ Yap and DR Carney, 'Preparatory Power Posing Affects Nonverbal Presence and Job Interview Outcomes' (2015), *Journal of Applied Psychology*, 100(4), 1286–95.

7 DY Hsu, L Huang, LF Nordgren, DD Rucker and AD Galinsky, 'The Music of Power, Perceptual and Behavioral Consequences of Powerful Music' (2015, January), *Social Psychological and Personality Science*, 6(1), 75–83.

Further reading

- R Branch and R Willson, *Cognitive Behavioural Therapy For Dummies*, 2nd edn (New York: John Wiley & Sons, 2010).
- M Williams and Danny Penman, *Mindfulness: A Practical Guide to Finding Peace in a Frantic World* (London: Piatkus, 2011).
- O Doyle, *Mindfulness Plain & Simple* (Watsonia, Australia: Doyle, 2011).
- Some universities now run mindfulness courses for their students, often via their counselling service.

Types of interview question

Contents

What you will learn in this chapter

As the diagram on the next page shows, there are many different types of interview question. This chapter introduces these types and teaches you strategies to handle these. The most common type of interview questions – competency questions – is such a large topic that it has a chapter all to itself.

Types of question

Open questions

Open questions are those which can't be answered with just 'yes' or 'no', such as *'Why do you want this job?'*, *'What do you know about our organization?'* and *'Why did you go to … university?'* These are the normal type of interview question and give you a chance to sell yourself. They start with Who, What, Where, When, Which, Why or How. Good open questions help you crystallize your thoughts and help the interviewer to understand your views, feelings and attitudes.

Closed questions

Closed questions can be answered with just 'yes' or 'no'. Examples include these: *'You studied law at university?'*, *'So, you did badly in your maths exams at school?'* and *'Are you a leader?'*

Types of interview question		
Question type	Comments	Example
Open	Can't be answered with just 'yes' or 'no'	*Why do you want this job?*
Closed/Leading	Can be answered with just 'yes' or 'no'	*You're bad at maths?*
Forced choice	Forces you to choose an answer	*Are you a leader or follower?*
Competency	Asks for evidence of skills in the job	*Describe a time where you worked in a team.*
Motivational	Checks that you've researched the job	*Who are our competitors?*
Biographical	Based on your CV	*What are your interests?*
Ethical	Tests honesty and integrity	*Is honesty always the best policy?*
Inappropriate	Illegal questions	*Will you have children?*
Technical	Technical and scientific questions	*How would you synthesize DNA?*
Cultural fit	Verifies that you fit the culture of the organization	*How do you feel about working long hours?*
Strengths-based	Focuses on your strengths	*What do you learn quickly?*
Hypothetical	'What if...' questions	*If you were a dog, what type would you be?*
Business case	Case study type questions	*How would you bring a new product to market?*
Market sizing	Estimates the market size	*How many lightbulbs are there in London?*
Puzzle	Logic puzzles or riddles	*Why don't polar bears eat penguins?*
Situational judgement	Work environment scenarios	*How would you deal with a customer making a complaint?*

Closed questions are asked by untrained interviewers. They limit information gathering, fail to explore possibilities and get too simple answers. If you give just a 'yes' or 'no' answer, you may be marked down as lacking in communication skills or, even worse, lack of interest in the job, so amplify your answers with, 'No, but ...' and 'Yes, and ...'. Develop your answer to show that you are articulate.

Example answers

You didn't do well in maths at school?

*No, I do admit that my grades weren't good, **but** I didn't put much effort in then as I didn't see the importance of maths back then. I had a part-time job which involved a lot of quick mental arithmetic, and I was surprised how easy I found this, and now I do understand the importance of maths. I put a lot of effort into my statistics module and gained a grade of 73 per cent which I was very proud of.*

You play hockey in your spare time?

Yes, and as you can see from my CV, I'm a keen hockey player at university. I play in defence and tend to organize the other players when we need to defend free hits or corners. I also get involved in the coaching of younger players, which I find very rewarding.

Leading questions are a type of closed question and tell you the answer the interviewer wants you to give! They are asked by untrained interviewers or occasionally by experienced interviewers who wish to put you on the spot:

● You're bad at languages, aren't you?
● So you didn't enjoy working there?
● So you can't use spreadsheets?

If you get asked about a particular skill you haven't got, then answer positively using 'No, but ...', as outlined above.

Example answer to 'So you can't use a spreadsheet?'

*No, I don't know how to use a spreadsheet, **but** I'm a quick learner and have taught myself how to use several other software applications, and I would really enjoy learning this, given a little training.*

Forced choice questions

Forced choice questions force you to choose an answer from two or more alternatives. They're designed to put you on the spot. Consider which attribute would be more needed in the job you are being interviewed for. For example if you are asked, *'Do you prefer to work on your own or in a team?'*, don't give the impression that you are capable of one, but not the other; instead, say that the role will dictate which aspect should take precedence. Programmers may spend much of their time working on their own, whereas for a marketing role, you would emphasize your team working skills. Here are other examples:

- Are you spontaneous or organized?
- Do you prefer to be right or to be liked?
- Would you rather know a lot about a little or a little about a lot? In other words, are you a specialist (researcher) or a generalist (manager)?

Are you a leader or a follower?

Both can have negative aspects. If you say you're a leader, you may be perceived as someone who always wants his or her own way and wouldn't make a good team member, but if you say you're a follower, you may be seen as someone who can't take the lead or think for him- or herself. You need a bit of both, but it also depends on the job. If you are applying for a trainee management role, you would need to show you were a leader, whereas for a backroom technical specialist role, it should be fine to say you are more of a follower.

Example answer

I prefer a leadership role as I like to drive things forward, but I do understand that there are times when you have to take more of a background role – to pull together as a member of the team. I know that when I start work, I will have a lot to learn and will need to take instruction from those with more knowledge and experience, but I hope to move quickly into a role where I can increasingly use my initiative.

Competency questions

These are the most common interview questions for large organizations and require you to give evidence of the qualities needed to perform well in the job. They have been given their own chapter (which follows this one) as it is a big topic.

Motivational questions

These questions check whether you have done your research on the job, organization and sector. See Chapter 1, 'Preparing for the interview', and Chapter 9, 'Try a practice interview'.

- Why do you want the job?
- Who else have you applied to? Your answer should include employers who are relevant (offering the same types of job), prestigious and in areas where you have been successful so far; don't mention those who have rejected you!
- Is contracting out public sector work to private sector firms a good thing?

Biographical questions

These are questions derived from your CV or application form. They check your education, employment and interests or ask about gaps in your CV such as an unexplained year.

- What grades did you get at A level?
- So you're studying law?
- What work experience have you had?
- What did you do in the year you took out before university? (Interviewers are happy for you to have taken a year out provided you've done something which stretched you, such as travel, voluntary work, fundraising for a charity or having a demanding job and developing skills. Talk enthusiastically about what you learned and how you developed as a person.)
- Tell me about yourself. (This is sometimes used as an icebreaker at the start of the interview. It's the perfect chance to put across your USPs [the attributes that make you right for the job], such as relevant skills, qualifications or experience. In one interview for a technology company, this was the only question asked. The poor interviewee was asked to go deeper and deeper and eventually ended up tying himself in knots.)

What are your interests?

This question allows you to convey your personality: who you are and what you enjoy doing. Talk about things that really fire your enthusiasm, as this will be picked up by the interviewer. Don't use clichés such as *'Socializing with friends'*, and try not to focus on potentially contentious areas such as politics and religion.

An interviewee with many solitary interests, such as reading, computer games and stamp collecting, might be perceived as unsocial. This might be okay for a job as a programmer but would give the wrong impression for marketing. If you do include these, talk about what you read or watch, and why.

> One environmental consultant looked for outdoor interests such as scuba diving or field sports when interviewing. This was because the work involved being outdoors in all weathers and times of year, and he found that people who didn't enjoy an outdoor lifestyle didn't stay long.

It's better to talk about a few interests and to show evidence of long-term commitment and in-depth involvement to these, as this suggests determination and dedication. For example, learning a musical instrument to grade 8 requires commitment and perseverance, and if you have regularly played in front of audiences, it also suggests you won't be fazed if you give a presentation. Listing many activities with just superficial involvement makes you appear a 'butterfly' – someone who flits between activities without commitment.

Talk about a range of interests as you don't want to appear narrow. If everything centres on sport, interviewers may wonder if you could hold a conversation with a client with no interest in this. I remember one finance graduate who talked just about her interest in business. When meeting colleagues or clients outside work, they won't just want to talk about work; they might want to discuss football, music or art, and if your interests are narrow, you may be perceived as boring.

Competitive sports can suggest the ability to handle pressure, and work in a team. Sports players earn more money on average because of the teamwork and leadership skills that sport develops. Skydiving or mountaineering can show a sense of wanting to stretch yourself and an ability to withstand pressure in demanding situations. Acting in a play requires teamwork and ability to work to a deadline, plus the ability to cope with pressure when on stage. Any group activities usually go down well.

> *If at first you don't succeed, then skydiving definitely isn't for you!*

Evidence of leadership, taking responsibility and initiative is important for most management roles: captain or coach of a sports team, course representative, chair of a student society or scout leader are all worth talking about.

Example answer to 'When have you shown leadership?'

As captain of my school cricket team, I had to set a positive example, motivate and coach players and think on my feet when making bowling and field position changes, often in tense situations.

Interests that are relevant to the job should be mentioned. Talk about your interest in current affairs if you wish to be a journalist, or your fantasy share portfolio if you want to work in finance. If you wish to be an events manager, you must mention events you've organized such as a fundraising event for a charity.

Hobbies that are out of the ordinary can help you to stick in the mind of the interviewer and stand out from the crowd: *'Oh yes, she's the candidate who teaches belly dancing.'* Talk about current interests as interviewers want evidence of your present ability to manage your time now and not how it was five years ago.

Example answers

I particularly enjoyed my role in the Air Cadet Force and learnt a lot about myself and the important things in life. I used my analytical problem-solving skills in practical situations under extreme pressure. I learnt about self-discipline, integrity, drive and determination, and the ability to persevere in challenging situations.

I play the guitar in a band currently performing in the local area. This requires a great amount of planning, teamwork and determination and culminated in our winning Battle of the Bands.

Travelling around Europe on my own developed my ability to be resourceful and adaptable, while enjoying meeting new people from all over the world.

During my Raleigh International Expedition to Ecuador I succeeded in the challenge of living and working in a completely different environment in a remote part of the world. It was a chance to discover more about myself, other people, team dynamics and different cultures and outlooks.

Ethical questions

These are asked in interviews for professions including medicine, law, finance and teaching, where integrity and honesty are paramount. You need to come across as a person with integrity but also one who has an understanding of the real-world implications. Here are some examples of typical questions:

- A 14-year-old girl comes to see you after finding out she is pregnant, but doesn't want her parents to be informed. What do you do? (medical school interview)
- Should the NHS waste money on treating people with self-inflicted problems such as obesity or smoking? (nursing interview)
- Is honesty always the best policy? (law interview)

Example answer to 'You think that a colleague is embezzling money; what do you do?' (asked at a finance interview)

I wouldn't jump to conclusions before I had gathered as much evidence as possible. No one should be accused of a crime without proof, as this could damage staff morale. I wouldn't confront the person directly as he or she might try to cover their tracks by destroying evidence. Once I was sure, I would talk privately with a manager, explaining what I had seen and allowing the manager to handle the situation.

Inappropriate and discriminatory questions

- Are you thinking of having children?
- Aren't you too old for this job?
- Are you planning to get married?
- Will you need time off for religious holidays?

Interviewers aren't allowed to ask questions about your religion, country of origin, parents or birthplace. They can't ask your age or your date of birth, and they are not allowed to ask your maiden name, marital status or about your children or partner's occupation, but they can ask if you are legally entitled to work in the UK.

You could get angry at such questions, but this would probably lose you the job. Such questions may be asked innocently by an untrained interviewer who is not aware of employment law. If you don't wish to answer, the best strategy is to stay calm and to politely ask the interviewer to explain the relevance of the question to the job. If the interviewer persists, you would be perfectly entitled to walk out – at least this may shock the interviewer into not asking the question to future candidates. Consider whether you want to work for such an unprofessional organization. If you feel you've been seriously discriminated against, contact the Equality and Human Rights Commission www.equalityhumanrights.com.

Technical questions

Technical questions are asked at interviews for computing, science, engineering and finance roles where your degree is directly related to the job and where the interviewer has a relevant technical background. If the interviewer isn't experienced, he or she may focus on your technical knowledge, feeling more comfortable asking questions about this.

Revise areas of your course that relate to the job. If you can't answer a question, tell the interviewer how you might go about solving the problem or where you would find the information you'd need to answer. Interviewers may prompt you and give you clues. They aren't only interested in your technical knowledge but also want to see how you reason and approach problems. Show that you can communicate technical information and ideas clearly and concisely to both people without a technical background and to experts in their field.

Sometimes a **funnelling technique** is used, where each question leads onto the next and is more specific. Questions start simple and broad and then drill down, becoming more specific and detailed, until you can't answer any further.

For example, a student applying for a post as a patent attorney was asked in order the questions below.

Example of the funnelling technique

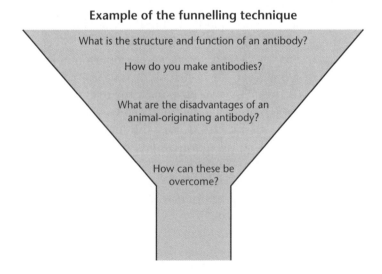

If at any point you couldn't answer, the interviewer would move onto another question.

It's common to be asked about course projects, especially group projects. Talk about your own role in the group, and say how you overcame any difficulties, for example, a group member who contributed little. You may be also asked about any dissertations you've done: how you chose these, how you carried out your research, problems you faced and how you overcame these. If asked about your project, the interviewer might ask the following questions:

- How did you choose your project? (Google, CGI, JP Morgan)
- How did you prepare it?
- How did you organize yourself?
- How did you do it?
- What did you learn from it?
- What did you enjoy about it?
- Justify the results.
- What would you do differently next time?

Example answer for 'Tell me about your project'

As the team leader of my group project with three other students, my planning and organizational skills came to the fore. We hosted a discussion at the University of Sussex for A-level students and teachers to give their views on ideas for refreshing business. I gained valuable experience in group presentation techniques and in managing my time. I learnt to work as part of a team, to communicate difficult concepts clearly and concisely and to write a report and work to tight deadlines. I achieved 76 per cent for this project, the highest mark in my year.

Some example technical questions asked at graduate interviews (answers are given later in the chapter)

1. What structure does NH2-CH2-COOH belong to? (biochemistry interview)
2. What do HIV and IgG stand for? (biology)
3. What is the polymerase chain reaction? (biology)
4. Why is the sky blue? (physics)

5. What is polarization? (physics)
6. What are constructive and destructive interferences? (physics)
7. What is stochastic modelling? (actuarial science)
8. What is polymorphism? (computing)
9. How many bytes is 2^{20}? (computing)

Sometimes questions which require in-depth problem solving will be asked, such as these:

- You are the manager at a production laboratory, and rising microbial counts have been observed going past acceptable levels in the water supply. How would you investigate and address this? (asked by a large pharmaceutical company)
- If you were organizing a future national breast screening campaign what standards, precautions, feasibility and practicality checks would you do? (asked at an interview for a medical physics post)

The technique used to answer these complex questions is similar to that used when answering hypothetical questions (see later in this chapter). Take a few seconds to think; then start with a few commonsense statements and gradually build your answer.

Answers to the above technical questions

1. NH2-CH2-COOH belongs to glycine (an amino acid).
2. HIV and IgG stand for human immunodeficiency virus and immunoglobulin G.
3. The polymerase chain reaction amplifies copies of a piece of DNA, generating millions of copies of a DNA sequence.
4. The sky is blue because air molecules scatter blue light from the sun more than they scatter red light.
5. The property of waves (such as light waves) that can oscillate with more than one orientation.
6. Constructive interference occurs when the phase difference between waves is a multiple of 2π, whereas destructive interference occurs when the difference is an odd multiple of π.
7. A stochastic model is a tool for estimating probability distributions of potential outcomes by allowing for random variation in one or more inputs over time.
8. Polymorphism is the ability of an object to take on many forms.
9. 2^{20} is 1048576 bytes.

Cultural fit questions

Cultural fit is about whether you will fit in with the organization: its methods of working, leadership, team styles and work culture (for example long hours and high rewards or better work life balance and lower rewards). For instance, the beauty company L'Oreal prefers confident, outgoing employees who are both creative and collaborative. Being able to fit in with the existing culture and teams can be more important to interviewers than skills and experience, as skills and experience can be acquired or enhanced through training, whereas personal attributes are harder to change. High-flying graduates may quickly lose their motivation if they don't fit in with the company's culture, work environment and values and so can't fully engage with the organization. Establishing the cultural fit of candidates is much harder than establishing their skills.

The biggest problem for organizations is defining their own culture in the first place. Company culture is often confused with the employer brand, core values and marketing, but the way the organization does things day to day doesn't match this. Value and mission statements come from the top, from senior management who have little contact with the real culture at the coalface, so these statements don't really represent the company's culture. Also different departments often have their own microcultures.

Typical cultural fit questions

What role do you normally play in a team?

Are you a leader, negotiator, compromiser, motivator, creative ideas person, clarifier and summarizer, analyser, initiator or listener? In an engineering company, analysers might rule the roost, whereas in an advertising agency creatives and persuaders might predominate. Of course, you need a mix of types in any good team. See Chapter 9, 'Try a practice interview', for more about team roles.

What makes a good employer?

You could focus on aspects such as being open to new ideas; being willing to listen to input from all employees, whatever their grade; and support for professional development and training.

Describe your preferred leadership style

Are you authoritarian or motivational? Do you lead by example? Are you laissez-faire, only intervening when there is a major problem?

Or are you democratic, giving everyone a chance to have a say? Or procedural, focusing mainly on procedures and tasks? Do you delegate? A graduate trainee with an authoritarian style would not lead successfully in a company with a more relaxed, inclusive style such as a university or law firm, but might do well in the armed forces, where quick decisions are vital. For more on leadership styles, see www.kent.ac.uk/careers/sk/leadership.htm.

What is the most important factor in your work environment for you to be productive and happy?

You could talk about your need for a defined work pattern and tasks, supportive colleagues, a busy schedule, a variety of work, a chance to be creative and to use initiative, autonomy, regular contact with clients or clearly defined targets.

Strengths questions

Strengths interviews have a simple aim: to find out your interests. Competency questions are the most common questions in graduate interviews and measure what you **can do** (your skills), whereas strengths interviews find out what you **enjoy doing**. By identifying your strengths and matching yourself to the role, you will enjoy it more and perform better than those who have to try hard to fill the role. You do more of what you are good at rather than what you are just capable of doing.

Strengths are the natural aptitudes people have for a role, such as analysing, organizing, taking responsibility and working with others. Strengths are innate, and when talking about their strengths, interviewees have more passion and sound more genuine, so the interviewer identifies your strengths by observing your energy and enthusiasm. From your body language and tone of voice, an interviewer can identify what you take pride in doing and when you have a genuine interest in a subject.

Some organizations such as Aviva, Standard Chartered, EY, Morrisons, Barclays, Nestlé, Royal Mail, BAE Systems and Unilever are moving away from competency interviews, as many applicants understand the formula too well and have well-rehearsed answers. In strengths interviews, interviewers get fewer pre-prepared answers from candidates, so get a more genuine insight into these candidates.

It increases the engagement of interviewers, and students enjoy the interview more, so they are more attracted to the organization. Applicants gain energy from the interview and can identify better whether they are suited for the role. Those recruited are more likely to stay in the job, perform better and learn faster.

Strengths interviews are especially useful for recruiting graduates who typically have limited work experience as interviewers are looking more for potential and passion for the job.

When people are using their strengths, they demonstrate 'flow': a real sense of energy and engagement. Time seems to fly by because they are so engrossed in the task, and they rapidly learn new information and approaches. People in a flow state are drawn to do things that play to their strengths even when tired, stressed or disengaged, and demonstrate high levels of performance.

You can't prepare for a strengths-based interview except by self-reflection. One of the beauties of strengths interviews is that you can't do much preparation and so are less likely to come up with hackneyed answers. Interviewees feel they've been better able to show who they are as a person rather than giving the same old answers to competency questions.

Think about what you love doing such as your hobbies and extracurricular activities and be open: don't try to be something you're not. Think of things you are proud to have done. Be honest about what tasks you don't enjoy doing, and think about how your preferences might fit with the organization's culture and the job requirements.

Questions asked at strengths interviews

- What are you good at?
- What comes easily to you?
- What do you learn quickly?
- What did you find easiest to learn at school or university?
- What subjects do you most enjoy studying?
- What things give you energy?
- Describe a successful day you have had.
- When did you achieve something you were really proud of?

- Do you prefer to start tasks or to finish them?
- Do you find you have enough hours in the day to complete all the things you want to do?
- What things are always left on your to-do list and not finished? (These are probably weaknesses – things you dislike doing.)
- What do you enjoy doing the least? (These are likely to be areas where you lack natural aptitude or skills.)

The interviewer will ask you questions around the above areas and ask for examples. Asking yourself the above questions will also help you to identify your strengths.

Hypothetical or curveball questions

The best curveball question I ever heard was in an interview for a major airline. *'What would you do if, after a long-haul flight, you found the pilot in the bar wearing a dress?'*

I'll let you think about how you would respond and give you the answer later on.

Curveball questions are unexpected, unusual and sometimes downright weird questions.

- Imagine you are in a plane falling from the sky without a parachute: What's good about it?
- Which four historical figures would you invite to dinner, and why?
- Describe yourself in five words.
- Describe the sky without using colours.
- Is a Jaffa Cake a cake or a biscuit?
- Who would win in a fight, Superman or Batman?
- You've won the lottery. What will you do with the money?

Why are they used?

Some interviewers pose hypothetical questions, also called 'curveball' questions. These are questions that you cannot anticipate. Interviewers are increasingly faced with 'textbook' answers to their questions as interviewees can now easily find help on how to answer common interview questions. This has created problems for interviewers. If interviewees give these pre-prepared answers, how can they really get to know the candidates?

Curveballs are used because it's impossible to work out your answer before the interview. They help interviewers discover the real candidate by bypassing your prepared answers, so they help an interviewer find out if you are capable of original thought and give a real feel for your personality. These hard questions may mean that the interviewer is interested in you and is putting you to a final test.

Many employers now use curveballs, including Google. Curveball questions are most commonly used by banks, consultancy firms and advertising agencies. They help the interviewer to find out answers to these questions:

- How do your thought processes work?
- Can you handle stress? Do you keep cool or get flustered?
- Can you think quickly and reason logically?
- Are you creative? Can you think outside the box?
- Do you have a sense of humour?
- How do you react to the unexpected?
- How well do you articulate your ideas?
- Can you develop practical solutions?

They also have disadvantages. Some interviewers ask these questions just to demonstrate how 'clever' they are. They can also breed resentment in interviewees. If they can't see how an interview question relates back to their ability to do the job, they may consider it unfair.

How do you answer?

Don't panic and blurt out your answer; instead, take a few seconds to think through the question. It's fine to say, *'That's a tough question. Do you mind if I think about it for a moment?'* The interviewer won't mind the silence; it will give the impression that you are thoughtful and are carefully considering your answer. Rather than weakness, this shows you have the confidence to act assertively.

Seek clarification if you need to. Ask the interviewer to repeat the question if you don't understand it completely. Again, this will give you more time to think. If your mind goes completely blank, ask if you can return to the question later. This doesn't demonstrate rapidity of thought, but the interviewer will appreciate the way you keep your composure.

There may be many possible solutions to the problem, and the interviewer won't expect a 'right' answer. What you actually say in your answer doesn't greatly matter as long as it sounds logical, demonstrates common sense and creativity, and shows an awareness of the issues involved. You could even suggest two solutions, with arguments for and against each. This would demonstrate a logical, structured approach to problem solving while avoiding committing yourself too soon to a single solution.

Don't try to form your whole answer in one go; just say one or two sensible things first. If you were asked how you would solve London's traffic problems, you could say that you would first carry out initial research and gather information from the main players. This gives you time to think further.

Think about why the interviewer might be asking the question. Does the job require quickness of thought, analytical skills and the ability to work under pressure or creativity? Relate your answer back to the job. If the job is a creative role, then an interviewer will want to see creativity in your response.

Smile and try to enjoy these questions. Be yourself: if you remain true to yourself and the interviewer still doesn't like your answer, it's probably not the right job for you.

You won't be able to predict these questions unless the interviewer lacks imagination and asks standard 'If you were a colour, what colour would you be?' type questions (see following). Practise answering some of the questions in this section to get used to thinking on your feet. You can find suggested answers to many such questions on the Web.

Let's look at the earlier question, *'What would you do if you found the pilot in the bar wearing a dress?'* The answer is to buy her a drink. Many airlines now recruit female pilots. The first one I remember joined British Airways after a degree in European Studies. You wouldn't fail the interview if you didn't realize that the pilot was female. It's an equal opportunities question, and they're just checking that you aren't narrow-minded.

A common example: If you were a colour, what colour would you be?

The interviewer is testing how you respond to unexpected situations: can you think on your feet? The interviewer is also examining your creativity. It's like a personality test: the interviewer is digging for personality traits. This is a silly question, but you have to play the interviewer's game if you want the job, so smile and give a good-natured answer rather than becoming irritated.

Pick a colour that exemplifies positive attributes that you have. Try to link your answer to your USPs or the skills the role requires. Red suggests dynamism; blue, calmness and logic; and yellow, a positive and optimistic nature. Ultimately, it doesn't matter which colour you choose, as long as you can justify it to the interviewer.

Here are some other variations:

• If you were an animal, what type of animal (or fruit/dog/dinosaur/biscuit/vegetable/car/book) would you be?	One candidate, when asked if she had any questions, asked the surprised interviewer, 'If you were a fruit, what kind of fruit would you be?' This question should be asked by the interviewer and *not* by the interviewee!
• Which historical/fictional/computer game character would you be? (Choose someone strong and dependable, with leadership qualities.)	
• Which three celebrities would you invite to a dinner party?	Another, with a coy smile, answered the colour question '50 shades of grey'!

Case questions

Case interview questions are asked in interviews for consultancy jobs, but also in interviews for jobs such as investment banking and law. You will also probably get standard interview questions alongside two or three case questions.

Case interviews involve the analysis of business problems and, unlike other interview questions, they are interactive. As well as being asked questions by the interviewer, you also have to ask the interviewer questions. It's fine to politely disagree with the interviewer – your assertiveness may impress them.

To answer case questions, you require the same skills a consultant needs: intelligence, analytical and logical reasoning skills, numeracy and ability to think creatively and flexibly. You also need 'helicopter ability', the ability to soar above a problem and see the big picture, but at the same time to be able to pay attention to the detail. These questions test your ability to solve problems under pressure and to present your recommendations in a reasoned and persuasive manner – quite a list!

The most common type of case question is the **business case**. You are given a business problem which you have to analyse and make recommendations on. Most case questions don't have just one answer. The point is to see whether you can think not only analytically but also laterally.

Occasionally, group interviews are used for these questions, where candidates work out a solution to a problem together, and sometimes they are presented on paper, especially if it's a complex question.

Examples:

- The company is considering outsourcing its present UK-based call centre to India. Is this a good idea, and why?
- McDonald's wants to open new branches in India. What problems might they face, and how would they solve these? (A key point here is that few Indians eat beef, so McDonald's India restaurants serve chicken or spiced potato burgers instead.)
- How would you bring a new product to market?
- The sales of our bestselling brand of washing powder are declining. How would you revive them?
- Sell me this cheap ballpoint pen! (See Chapter 6, 'Interviews for different roles', for an answer.)
- A company makes profits for three successive quarters and then makes a 40 per cent loss in the next quarter compared to the same quarter last year. Why might this be?

- I'm an alien from outer space, who has just landed on Earth. Succinctly describe Britain's transport system (asked by transport company).

Market-sizing questions

Market-sizing questions require you to estimate the market size for a product. The trick to answering involves making careful guestimates of the size of the market. You aren't given factual information, so at first sight, these questions may seem impossible but the interviewer isn't expecting an accurate answer – you aren't expected to be an expert. They are looking for your ability to make quick mental approximations and to extrapolate from what you do know when accurate data isn't given. Try answering the following two questions, and we'll give you the solutions later.

- How many lightbulbs are there in London? (asked by an investment bank)
- How many basketballs can you fit in this room? (asked by a computing company in a typical interview office)

Other market-sizing questions which have been asked:

- How many piano tuners are there in the United Kingdom?
- How many footballs would fit inside a jumbo jet?
- How many cars are there in Germany?
- How many phones are there in the United States?

Tips for market-sizing and case questions

- These questions are complex, so you need to take your time and to think logically. Listen carefully to the interviewer and ask him or her to repeat anything you don't understand – this will also give you more time to think. Also say, 'That's a good question. May I have a few moments to think about it?'
- Look at the big picture at the start, and then drill down to the specific details.
- First break down the question into the facts that you need to guestimate. You may be given a pen and paper to note facts, make

calculations and to structure your answer, but you won't usually be able to use a calculator.

- Bring a watch, pen and pad and a calculator, just in case you are allowed to use one.
- Take notes whilst the interviewer is outlining the problem. This is one interview situation where it's okay to write things down, but do ask the interviewer's permission first.
- You probably won't be given the full picture at the start, so ask the interviewer for clarification of any aspects where insufficient information has been given.
- If you can't use a calculator, round numbers up or down to within 10 per cent. For this type of question 1000 is nearly the same as 958 or 1045.
- Work in metric – metres and kilograms are easier to calculate than yards and pounds.
- Think out loud and present your thinking in a clear and logical manner, briefly summarizing your conclusions at the end.

How many lightbulbs are there in London?

First, you would need to guess the population of London – say 8 million. A typical house contains, say, five individuals and perhaps has 20 lightbulbs, perhaps one for each room, some for wall lights, torches and spares. This makes about 4 lightbulbs for each person living in London = 4 x 8 million = 32 million. But we also need to account for lights used by businesses, street lamps, sports stadiums, and so on. We could add another 50 per cent for this, for example 16 million more. This gives a total of 48 million.

Consider if your answer makes sense. If your answer for the number of lightbulbs was 1 million, you would have made a mistake somewhere, so check your analysis. It's fine to use creativity in your answers as long as they are also logical. Key skills looked for are the ability to structure, to think laterally and make links, and to give a logical answer.

How many basketballs could you fit in this room?

Firstly, you would estimate the size of the room. Say 5 m x 4 m x 3 m for a typical room. Then you need to estimate the diameter of a basketball – say, 25 cm, so four basketballs would fit into one metre. So the amount of basketballs would be 20 x 16 x 12 = 192 x 20 = 3840. This is, of course, if they were stacked vertically above each other. Perhaps another 5 per cent could be fitted in if they were tessellated (stacked diagonally).

Don't be afraid to ask questions. Here you would need to ask the interviewer if he or she meant with the furniture in the room or not and then adjust your calculations accordingly.

Make sensible estimates by rounding numbers up or down. For example, if you thought that the size of a basketball was 23 cm, rounding this to 25 cm would make your mental calculations much easier and not significantly change the result.

Puzzle questions

Puzzle questions are normally riddles or logic puzzles and sometimes test your factual knowledge. Again they test your analytical reasoning but also your ability to think laterally. You need to be good at maths for some of these questions! They are normally asked in interviews for jobs that require high levels of analysis or creativity.

Examples (answers are given later in the chapter)

1. If you had 2385 participants in a tournament, how many games would need to be played to determine the winner? (asked by an international book company)
2. How many degrees are there between clock hands at 3.15? (asked by an investment bank)
3. How many cubes are exposed in a Rubik's Cube?
4. A man pushed his car to a hotel and lost his fortune. Why? (asked by Google)
5. How do you cut a cake into eight pieces with three straight cuts?
6. Why are manhole covers round instead of square?
7. Why don't polar bears eat penguins?
8. In many London Underground tube stations, why are there two escalators going up but only one going down?

9. How can you throw a ball as hard as you can, and make it stop and return to you, without hitting anything and with nothing attached to it?

10. The amount of water flowing into a tank doubles every minute. The tank is full in an hour. When is the tank half full?

11. What is the next letter in this sequence: J F M A M J?

12. A woman was born in 1968 but only recently celebrated her 12th birthday. Why?

13. What can you put in a wooden box that would make it lighter? The more of them you put in, the lighter it becomes, yet the box stays empty.

14. A black man dressed all in black, wearing a black mask, stands at a crossroads in a totally black-painted town. All of the streetlights in town are broken. There is no moon. A black-painted car without headlights drives straight toward him, but turns in time and doesn't hit him. How did the driver know to swerve?

15. There is an ancient invention still used in most parts of the world today that allows people to see through walls. What is it?

16. A child lives on the tenth floor of a block of flats. Every morning she takes the lift down to the ground floor and goes to school. In the evening, she gets into the lift, and if there is someone else in the lift, she goes back to her floor directly. Otherwise, she goes to the eighth floor and walks up two flights of stairs to her parents' flat. How do you explain this?

Situational judgement questions

Situational judgement questions allow interviewers to gain an idea of your decision-making and problem-solving skills within the relevant work environment. They are used by many companies, including Accenture, PWC, Transport for London and McDonald's. They give you a clear understanding of the role and kind of work situations you may meet. They present you with a short scenario you might experience in the job you are applying for, and you must decide the best action to take. Questions often start with, 'What would you do if …?' or 'How would you deal with …?'

These questions are often ambiguous, with more than one possible solution. Use logic and common sense when answering, and remember: the customer always comes first! Show tact in dealings with customers and clients. Your solution should never solely be 'I would ask the manager what to do' as this would suggest a lack of initiative and ability to take responsibility. If you have worked in customer service environments such as shops or restaurants, you may already have an understanding of how to deal with similar situations, based on your experience. Here are some examples.

- What would you do if a team member was not pulling his or her weight on a group task?
- How would you deal with a colleague whom you caught stealing?
- An angry customer comes into the shop you work in, asking to return a microwave she bought five months ago that has stopped working. The person says she can't find her receipt. The shop has a policy of replacing the item or giving a full refund only up to 60 days after purchase. What do you do?

Example answer to microwave question

I would keep calm and say that I understood the customer's annoyance and quickly apologize. I would find out the full details, and if I couldn't sort it out myself, ask the customer to come with me to consult the manager so that she could make a decision. I would say that I would do my utmost to ensure the customer went away satisfied today, either with a replacement item or with a guarantee to have it repaired. I have listened carefully to the customer and apologized to her and am demonstrating to her that I am doing my best to come to a resolution.

NASA spent millions of dollars developing a pen for astronauts that could write in space. The Russians used a pencil.

Answers to the puzzle questions

1. The answer is 2384. In a knockout tournament, every team except the winner is defeated once and once only, so the number of matches is one less than the number of teams in this case 2385 – 1 = 2384.

2. The answer is not zero degrees as you might at first think. The minute hand will be at 15 minutes (90 degrees clockwise from vertical), but the hour hand will have progressed to one-quarter of the distance between 3 p.m. and 4 p.m. Each hour represents 30 degrees (360/12), so one-quarter of an hour equals 7.5 degrees, so the minute hand will be at 97.5 degrees: a 7.5 degree difference between the hands.

3. A Rubik's Cube has 3^3 cubes = 27 cubes. Only one of these (the one right at the centre) is not exposed so the answer is 26 cubes.

4. He was playing Monopoly!

5. Divide the cake into quarters with two vertical cuts and then make the third cut horizontal through the cake.

6. Manhole covers are round so that they can't fall through the hole. If they were square, they could fall through the diagonal of the hole.

7. Polar bears don't eat penguins because polar bears live near the North Pole and penguins near the South Pole, so the only time they will ever meet is in a zoo!

8. People leave trains in a group, so all arrive at the escalators at the same time but tend to go down to the trains in a more even flow; hence you need less down escalators.

9. Go outside and throw it upwards.

10. It is half full just one minute before it is full at 59 minutes.

11. J (for July). They are the first letters of the months of the year.

12. She was born on February the 29th.

13. Holes

14. It was daytime.

15. The window

16. The child is small and couldn't reach the upper lift buttons.

Finding out more

On the companion website www.palgravecareerskills.com

- Example answers to many more questions

On the Web

- **From What is Wrong to What is Strong:** the psychology of strengths interviews www.positivepsychology.org.uk/pp-theory/strengths/112-from-what-is-wrong-to-what-is-strong.html
- **Quiz on being assertive in interviews** University of Kent www.kent.ac.uk/careers/assertiveness.htm

Chapter 4

How to STAR at competency questions

Contents

- What are competency questions?
- The STAR approach
- Example answers using STAR
- Exercise: Prepare your own STAR answer

What you will learn in this chapter

- Why competency questions are so common
- What they are, how to identify them and why employers use them
- How to identify your employability skills and the evidence you can give to an employer to show you have these
- How to identify the competency questions you might be asked for different roles
- How to give strong structured answers to these questions using the STAR approach

> **How not to answer competency questions:**
>
> 66 Working on a farm has improved my communication skills, which are especially important when working with large livestock. 99

Competency questions are just another type of interview question, but they have been given their own chapter as they are normally the most common and most important questions asked in interviews, and the varied techniques used to answer these questions warrant a chapter of their own.

The advert just said 'Good teamworking skills required'.

Bruce Woodcock

What are competency questions?

Competency just means a skill or ability. Competencies are the key skills organizations look for in staff as they are linked to successful performance. Competency-based questions are the most common questions in graduate interviews and are the hardest part of the interview for many applicants. These questions work on the theory that past experience is the basis for future performance and so ask for examples of what you have done that will give the interviewer evidence that you've got the necessary skills to succeed in the job.

To get a graduate job, you need the right skills to do it. To be successful, you must identify the skills you're good at and present evidence to show you hold these skills at interview.

Advantages and disadvantages

Competency interviews can seem impersonal as you don't get much opportunity for discussion; when you've answered the question, the interviewer will move on to another competency. Interviewees are asked the same questions in the same order, often with a range of follow-up questions. As all candidates are asked the same questions, it reduces the chance of subjectivity, especially when a number of interviewers are assessing many candidates.

Competency interviews are reliable, objective and consistent, but techniques to answer the questions can be learnt. Because many organizations use competency questions in application forms, at interview some applicants know the formula too well. They carefully rehearse their answers to questions, so the interviewer doesn't see the 'real' candidate. Some employers such as EY are therefore moving away from competency-based recruitment.

Similar competency questions are often asked on application forms and at interview, so the best way to prepare for a competency interview is to read the answers you've given to competency questions on application forms.

Skills in competency interviews

Graduate recruiters focus their selection on the core skills required in the job they are recruiting for. The employer analyses the skills needed in the job, especially those possessed by high-performing staff in the role. They then base their interview questions around these competencies which are essential for success in that job.

> 'You need to be very well prepared with examples of teamwork, leadership, planning, responsibility, communication etc.'
>
> Student interviewed by an accountancy firm

There is a grid of criteria (see the person specification in Chapter 1, 'Preparing for the interview'), with questions that relate to those criteria, and the interviewer writes down the evidence that shows you meet those criteria after each question. Each question is given a score, and the candidate with the highest total score succeeds, so you must learn to relate the skills you have to those needed in the job.

Improving your skills

You can improve your skills, and in fact a key skill that interviewers look for is the ability to assess what you are good at and where your weaknesses lie and then to remedy any weaknesses that might affect your performance in the job. This involves being able to self-analyse and reflect. This is one reason that the question *'What are your weaknesses?'* is so common at interview. See Chapter 9, 'Try a practice interview', for help answering this question.

By improving one skill, you will also improve others. By improving your persuasiveness, you will also improve your ability to negotiate and to lead.

Skills map

The following map of skills outlines most of the soft skills required in graduate jobs. As you can see, they are in related groups. For example, leadership requires you to motivate, delegate and make decisions. Some skills overlap: for example influencing includes the skills of persuading and negotiating. Spoken communication has many facets including listening, persuading and presenting to an audience. Which are your strongest skills and which do you need to improve?

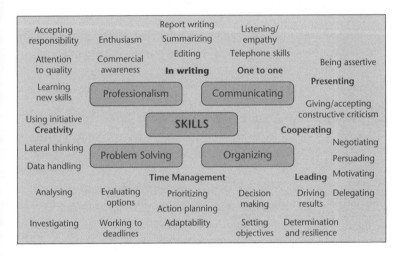

Informative but concise answers

Each question assesses you against set criteria such as your ability to work in a team, so work out which of these criteria a particular question pertains to, and address that. If you don't focus on the important, then the unimportant will take precedence.

Have a variety of examples from different contexts: academic, extracurricular, work, and so on. Don't take all of your examples from academic environments, for example coping with pressure in exams or time management when revising, as this suggests you have little real-world experience. If you have a strong example such as a relevant placement, it's fine to use this twice, but use different aspects of the role for each answer. It's also okay to reuse some of the same examples you used in your application form, but give your answer from a different perspective or include different detail.

As well as looking at what you say, recruiters will look at how you say it, including your use of English and how well you express yourself.

Different jobs need different skills

Some skills such as team working and communication are common to many careers. Other skills such as leadership and technical skills are more specific. Each job requires a unique suite of skills.

- **Teachers** must be good at **presenting** in front of the class; to be good **listeners**; to understand the reasons why a bright student is not progressing; and able to **organize** the syllabus for the next term.
- **IT consultants** must be able to **ask** their clients the right questions, to deduce their requirements. They need to be able to **analyse** these requirements, **present** their solutions to the client and **persuade** him or her that their preferred solution is the right one.

Key attributes required for some graduate jobs			
Teacher	presenting	listening	organizing
Social worker	speaking	cooperating	empathy
Nurse	cooperating	adaptability	organizing
Journalist	writing	investigating	listening
Scientist	analysing	investigating	problem solving
Software engineer	analysing	logical thinking	problem solving
Accountant	advising	investigating	numeracy
Marketing manager	persuading	negotiating	lateral thinking
Barrister	presenting	persuading	writing
HR manager	advising	negotiating	listening

How do I identify competency questions?

Questions usually begin with statements such as **'Describe a time or situation when you ...'** or **'Give an example of ...'** and then ask for examples of specific skills such as communication or leadership.

Examples of specific skills

> *One interviewee for a banking job, when asked about relevant qualifications, talked about his certificate in heavy lifting.*

- **Writing:** *Describe a situation where you conveyed ideas or facts to others clearly through writing.*
- **Negotiating:** *Give an example of when you negotiated a solution to a conflict of opinions.*
- **Leading:** *Tell me about a time when you demonstrated leadership.*
- **Presenting:** *Give an example of when you made a presentation to a group of people.*
- **Organizing and planning:** *Describe a time when your organization resulted in the successful achievement of a task.*
- **Making decisions:** *Give an example of a major decision you have taken and how you arrived at it.*
- **Withstanding pressure:** *Tell me about a time when you worked under pressure to complete a task.*
- **Exceeding expectations:** *Describe a situation when you went out of our way to satisfy someone's expectations.*
- **Analysing:** *Give an example of when you analysed complex information to extract the essential points.*
- **Adaptability:** *Describe a situation when you adapted to changing situations.*
- **Problem solving:** *Describe a situation when you devised an innovative solution to a problem.*
- **Determination:** *Describe a situation when you succeeded in a challenging task in difficult circumstances.*
- **Time management:** *Tell me about a time when you managed a number of conflicting priorities.*
- **Teamwork:** *Describe a situation when you worked effectively in a team to accomplish a task.*
- **Persuading:** *Describe a time when you convinced somebody to do something that they were initially reluctant to do.*

Debbie's story

The role I was interviewed for was customer facing, and I was asked questions based on my experiences with customers, so make sure you understand the role and the key skills it needs. Most of the questions were along the lines of 'Give an example of when you dealt with a difficult customer, went the extra mile for a customer, had a problem on a project or made a hard decision.' You have to be well prepared with examples of teamwork, communicating and similar skills. Make sure you have prepared answers, even if it is just in your head, as the interviewer won't be looking for scripted answers. Think carefully about the things you have done in your life and how you can use them to show your strengths. Prepare a lot of examples when you have shown any skills or leadership, and be able to talk about each one for a few minutes.

Debbie, graduate in English literature interviewed for graduate programme in retailing

The STAR approach

The best way to structure your answer is via the STAR approach – **S**ituation, **T**ask, **A**ction and **R**esult. Using STAR will give your answers a clear structure and logical progression. Your answer then becomes a short story about yourself with a beginning, middle and ending which flows nicely.

- The **Situation and Task** combine to form the introduction.
- The **Action** you took forms the main body of your answer and is the longest part.
- The **Result** is your conclusion and is quite short.

It's like a story. For each situation, say what happened, how you approached it and what the outcome was. Your answers could come from vacation or part-time jobs, university societies, voluntary work, academic study, holidays and travel or personal experiences. Don't take all the examples from academic studies, as employers want evidence that you are a rounded individual.

As a rule of thumb, your STAR answers should take about two minutes. The situation and task might take you about 30 seconds to describe; the actions you took might take about 60 seconds; and the result, another 30 seconds.

Situation/Task	Action	Result
About 30 seconds	About 60 seconds	About 30 seconds

The Situation and Task

This forms the introduction and sets the scene. You describe the scenario and task you were faced with: the date and place – when, where and with whom. Think of relevant examples rather than the most impressive. Talk about a specific event or situation rather than giving a general description of what you've done. If you are asked to describe a time when you had to give a presentation, a seminar paper which involved research and planning will carry more weight than *'presenting flowers to the Queen when I was 13'*.

Don't make the mistake of going into too much background detail about the situation and task. Keep it short and to the point: What was the skill? What was the task? What did you set out to achieve? Was there a timescale?

The Action

Show that you decided what had to be achieved and then took logical steps towards your goal. There should be more than one action, or your answer will be thin. This will be the longest part of your answer, where you describe in detail what you did.

- What was your approach to achieving it? Why did you adopt this approach?
- How and why were decisions made?
- What were the tasks?
- How did you convince others to buy into your idea?
- Did you have to explain complex information to someone in a simple way?
- Did you accept suggestions from others?
- What problems did you face, and how did you overcome these?
- What skills did you use to solve any problems that arose?

- Did you have to juggle priorities to meet a deadline?
- If things went wrong, did you remain positive and show evidence of resilience and determination?

The interviewer may ask you to explain particular bits in more depth or to justify how you did things.

If it was a **group task**, use 'I', not 'we'. What action did *you* personally take? The focus should be on you. Even if the situation involved a group, interviewers want to know your specific role in achieving the result. Keep the focus on yourself, your role in the team and your own contribution to the outcome.

- Who else was in the team?
- How did you interact with the other members?
- How were the individuals different?
- What challenges did you face working with them?
- Did you respect different perspectives?
- Did you adapt your approach to work with others who had different personalities?
- How did you help keep everyone focused and motivated to achieve the goal?

Interviewers will look for evidence of motivation, enthusiasm, teamwork, leadership, communication skills and your ability to learn from mistakes. They will also be assessing your determination and resilience: did you pick yourself up and carry on when there was a setback, find another way round the problem or just give up?

Action words

Use action words in your answers. Action words are active, positive words which give your answers additional impact. Action words give an impression of a positive, motivated person who knows how to present him or herself in a professional manner and who will succeed in a variety of work areas, whereas passive words and phrases such as *used to, had to, was told to, tried to, was involved in* and *went* suggest the opposite. Also beware of negative words such as *bad, hate* and *mistake.*

Here are some common action words:

Which of the following has more impact?

1. For my project I had to do a survey of people, in which they filled in a questionnaire and I got a good mark.
2. For my project I **planned** and then **designed** a questionnaire which I then **persuaded** 50 people to complete. I **presented** my results to a panel and **achieved** a grade of 78 per cent.

1. As a sales assistant, I had to serve customers, handle cash, maintain stock levels and was told to look after the store in the absence of the manager.
2. As a sales assistant, I was **responsible for** advising customers, **resolving** any problems that arose and **organizing** my work and stock control. This **required me** to handle large amounts of cash and **ensure** that a correct balance was achieved. I was **entrusted** with sole **responsibility** for the shop in the absence of the manager.

Beware buzzwords!

Beware of buzzwords, those vapid expressions such as *'I'm a dynamic team player with a track record of success'* that interviewers hear time and time again. These are typically not backed up by evidence and so have no value. Typical buzzwords are *dynamic, passionate, results-oriented, entrepreneurial* and *driven*. Similarly, words such as *diligent, punctual, hard-working, reliable* and *team player* may make you sound a little boring.

Don't say this:

I'm a dynamic, passionate and motivated team player with a proven track record and a unique strategic vision allowing me to increase leverage by paradigm shifts to push the envelope forward. (**no evidence supplied**)

Do say this:

I have developed strong organizational and problem-solving skills through my involvement with Rag fundraising and promotional work in vacations. I successfully combined my studies with work and other commitments, showing myself to be self-motivated and able to work under pressure and to effectively manage my time. (**evidence-based**)

The Result

Employers want candidates who achieve results and make a difference. Your result should be short and positive. Was it a success? What positive impact did your actions lead to? What changed as a result of your efforts? If the result was negative, say what you learned from the experience and what you would do differently next time.

Try to give quantifiable results:

● *We raised £300 for charity.*
● *My project was awarded a grade of 75 per cent.*
● *Membership rose by 20 students.*

You can't always do this, but it gives a better idea of your achievement.

Being asked to reflect

Employers expect graduates to be able to reflect on and learn from their experiences. This is why they ask questions about your weaknesses at interview; they are finding out if you learn and grow from your failures or keep repeating the same old mistakes. Some organizations have now added **Reflection** (What have you learned from the experience and what would you do differently next time?) to give STARR. How might you have done things differently? What did you learn about yourself and others? Did this learning help you to grow in any way?

Example answers

I learnt that I am successfully able to work in a team but also take control when need be. I also learnt that people like to feel included and to be given a part to play.

I learnt that people who don't know each other could create something that will help the community.

I learnt that communication is the key. I should have phoned my colleagues to check on their progress more regularly.

Despite the difficult group I was in, I discovered I was capable to reach my goals when determined enough – a positive attitude and hard work took me further than hostility.

On reflection, I would allow for more time before the event, to allow for potential problems to be corrected in good time.

I have learned how to efficiently relay information, especially about new and unfamiliar concepts.

Bullet your answers

Before your interview, write down the key points to your answers in bullet form. Don't try to memorize your whole answer verbatim, as this would sound false. For example:

Situation and Task

- Group project in final year at university

Action:

- Role as group leader
- Organized regular meetings in library
- Problem with group member who wasn't contributing and how this was solved
- Completed well before deadline due to good planning

Result:

- Awarded grade of 68 per cent

Probing Questions

The initial question may be followed up by more probing questions to gather more detailed information and to check for distortions or lies. If you say, *'During my time as chairman, membership rose by 100 per cent'*, an alert selector will probe you about the size of the society and may find out that you were the only member and that during the year, you recruited your best mate, thus doubling the number of members.

You are asked a series of questions, each focusing more deeply on the same area, forcing you to explain in more detail. The questions use the words *who, what, how, when* and *why*. A funnelling technique is used, where each question leads onto the next and is more specific. Questions start simple and broad and then drill down, becoming more detailed, until you can't answer any further. In the following examples, the initial question is given first, and the probing questions follow.

1. **Give an example of a situation when you demonstrated resilience to reach a goal.**
2. What was the goal?
3. What made it challenging?
4. Describe any setbacks and obstacles and how you overcame these.
5. What was the result?

1. **Give an example of a time you worked in a team.**
2. What was your role in the team?
3. What action did you personally take?
4. What was the outcome?
5. What impact did you have on the result?
6. What did you learn from the experience?
7. What might you do differently next time?

1. **Describe a situation where you had a problem when you worked in a team.**
2. When did this happen?
3. What role did you take in the team?
4. How did you deal with the problem?
5. What was the result?
6. What could you have done better?
7. How could you stop it reoccurring?

1. **Talk about a time when you had to make an important decision.**
2. What was the decision?
3. What information did you have available?
4. How did you identify the important factors?

5. How did you decide what priority to give these factors?
6. What risks did you take into account?
7. What impact did your decision have?

Example answers using STAR

Describe a **SITUATION** where you used communication skills.	
On a busy day, I was on the customer service desk at ASDA. A lady was very unhappy with some food she had bought for Christmas dinner which she said had proved inedible. I therefore had to resolve this and ensure the customer left satisfied.	Shows he can work under pressure.
What **ACTION** did you take?	
I used the procedure I had been taught in training, which involved me calming the customer down and empathizing with her situation. **I assured her that I fully understood her feelings and explained how this could have occurred, whilst knowing that this would be poor consolation.** I stated that she was entitled to a full refund and the same item free. To ensure she left satisfied, I gave her a goodwill voucher for £10 to make up for the inconvenience. I told her that we would **take extra care to ensure there would be no repetition** and thanked her for her understanding.	Action is the largest part of the answer. Evidence of tact and sensitivity. Prevents future problems.
What was the **RESULT?**	
After I finished serving her, she demanded to see my manager. I was worried that she would complain, but to my delight, **she praised me.** She said how calm and efficient I had been when resolving the situation, especially considering how busy I was.	Impressive result.
What did you **LEARN?**	
I learnt that you need to **listen carefully** to people and that a **friendly smile** goes a long way!	Nice touch of humour, but also very true.

Describe a SITUATION where you worked effectively in a team	
For a course module, I worked with five other students on a **group essay** and presentation.	Group projects normally make good teamwork examples.
What ACTION did you take?	
We first arranged a group meeting in which specific tasks were assigned to each member so that all parts would be drafted simultaneously to save time. **We arranged regular meetings** in the library to research our topic and to share knowledge. We began compiling the questionnaire and the corresponding elements of the presentation as we completed them. **We agreed a deadline** for completion of drafts and then met to redraft the final version together. I was responsible for the last part of the essay but also **acted as group leader** suggesting the location and times for meetings, setting deadlines and **encouraging group members who fell behind**. We aimed to complete both the essay and the presentation a week before the presentation in order to practise presenting together and to suggest improvements to each other's parts. It was vital to keep making progress and I made sure each person had tasks to do before the next meeting.	Action is the largest part of the answer.

Good planning and organization.

Evidence of good time management.

Interviewers like to see evidence of leadership skills.
Clearly defines her role. |
What was the RESULT?	
Due to our efficient time management, we submitted the essay well before the deadline and received a grade of **86 per cent** for our presentation, the highest in the year. All members of the group were equally involved and learnt vital skills, including research and presenting skills.	Quantifiable result.
What did you LEARN?	
I learnt that all groups need leadership, but ultimately the group effort is most important, and by working together, we can generate a better result.	Learns from experience.

Exercise: Prepare your own STAR answer to a teamwork question

Describe a situation when you worked in a team to achieve a demanding goal?

Teamwork questions are the most common competency questions in interviews. Your answer should be about 250 words in total as this is about the length of a typical answer at interview. Once you have completed this, show your answer to a friend and ask them what they think.

The situation and task. What was the task? What did you set out to achieve? Was there a timescale? Think of examples from your course, activities such as student societies, school, work or travel.

What action did you take? This will be the longest part of your answer. Say in detail what you actually did. What was your approach to achieving it? Why did you adopt this approach? How and why were decisions made? Did you have to convince others to buy into your plan? What obstacles did you have to overcome, and how did you do this?

What was your own contribution and role in the team?

What was the result? Was it a success? What changed as a result of your efforts? Can you quantify your result?

What did you learn? How might you have done things differently? What did you learn about yourself and others?

Finding out more

On the companion website www.palgravecareerskills.com

- Example answers to more questions

On the Web

- **Action words slot machine** University of Kent www.kent.ac.uk/careers/cv/actionverbs.htm

Types of interview

What you will learn in this chapter

- The different types of interview, including those with more than one interviewer
- How group interviews and second interviews differ from standard interviews

How many interviewers?

The single interviewer

In larger organizations, the interviewer will probably be from the HR department, but in a smaller organization this person may be a manager from the department you would be joining. In this case, the manager may not be a trained interviewer and may not ask the standard interview questions.

Two-to-one interviews

These typically involve an HR manager and a line manager from the function for which you are applying. This can be more demanding as the questions come from two people, so you may have less time to think.

Panel interviews

In panel interviews, you are interviewed by three or more interviewers representing different areas of the organization. Panel interviews are more prevalent in the public sector, where you could be faced with five or six interviewers. Because of the expense involved, panel interviews are more common for senior roles, with junior jobs decided by one-to-one interviews. I would seriously question the efficiency of any organization that pulled six staff from their work to interview an applicant for a junior post.

Panels are becoming more common as companies look for more rigorous ways to screen candidates. They can also save an organization time but are more formal, and it can be difficult to establish a rapport with the interviewer.

When you enter, look at all the interviewers, and introduce yourself to each member of the panel. Remember names if you can. Engage the whole panel and not just one specific interviewer. The only real difference from a one-to-one interview is that when you're asked a question you should keep eye contact with the person asking the question, but when you answer, scan the whole panel from time to time. This shows that you're confident, and it will build a rapport with the whole panel.

Some panel members may not be experienced interviewers and may not always ask appropriate questions or may repeat questions other interviewers have already asked. There may be a chairperson who asks most of the questions, or different panel members may be responsible for different aspects of the interview, the HR manager asking competency questions and a line manager asking technical questions. Panel members may have their own agenda, one playing good cop, being friendly, and another taking the role of bad cop by asking tough questions.

Panel interviews can be challenging as they put you under pressure, with questions fired in from the left, right and centre; these questions can show how you might cope in a demanding role. The most challenging type is the free-for-all, with panel members asking questions at random.

Group interviews

Group interviews are used to quickly reduce a lot of candidates to a manageable number. You may be asked to briefly introduce yourself to the other candidates, or each interviewee may be asked several questions. They are a good way of eliminating candidates who aren't comfortable in groups and so are often used in interviews for jobs where group work skills are important, such as teaching.

> *The secret of doing well at a group interview is to try to enjoy it! It will be demanding but will also be fun, and the candidates who put the most in will get the most out of it.*
>
> Retail company

Tips

The interviewers are looking for enthusiasm and confidence in group situations and also observing what roles you take in the group: leader, ideas person, summarizer and clarifier, or analyst. See Chapter 9, 'Try a practice interview' for more on team roles.

Don't put on a façade; be yourself. The other interviewees will also be nervous; chat to them in breaks or make small talk with the interviewers as this will make you more relaxed. The interviewers will also be observing who is being genuinely friendly and who is hiding in a corner. Take a highlighter pen to highlight key points on any information sheets given for group exercises.

Speak clearly, loud enough for everyone to hear. In one group interview for the Civil Service, the selectors sitting in the corners had problems assessing the candidates because they were talking so softly.

You may be asked to discuss pertinent issues. For example a question such as *'How would you make Shakespeare interesting to a group of mixed ability 14-year-old boys?'* might be asked in a group interview for teaching.

Listen to the views of others, and support those you agree with. Don't put down other group members: you're not usually competing directly against the other members of the group; everyone could be selected or everyone rejected.

If a group member is quiet, try to get this person to contribute: *'We haven't heard from Mina yet – I'd like to hear her views.'*

Tips from students

The biggest thing that gave me confidence was the realization that everyone else was nervous; the other candidates were very friendly with each other in general. I took it as an opportunity to chat to people in the breaks, and I actually forgot I was probably being assessed as I was enjoying myself. I also found it helped to make small talk with the interviewers.

One or two of the candidates tried too hard to impress and were very overbearing when it came to the group exercises. I'm not sure that this is what the assessors were looking for, and it certainly didn't make them popular with the other candidates.

Go for quality rather than quantity in your contributions; don't rabbit on. Candidates who make active and thoughtful contributions are preferred. Stick up for your opinions, arguing logically and persuasively for them, and introduce new ideas or build on the ideas of others.

Be assertive and use your sense of humour. If a bossy person tries to take control, challenge him or her, but in a calm and reasoned manner: *'What are your reasons for saying that?'*

If you are made leader of an exercise, delegate responsibility, asking for volunteers for tasks such as note taking. Identify the strengths of your team and use them. Don't get involved in the detail of the task: as leader you have to keep the broad view.

Second interviews

Why are second interviews used?

Second interviews are held to assess you more thoroughly and get a second opinion. Around 30 per cent of first interviewees are offered second interviews, so if you've got this far, it suggests you're a good match for the job and that your interview skills are strong.

Who holds second interviews?

Usually large graduate recruiters have a second interview stage, with smaller organizations often interviewing just once.

Who will interview me?

Initial interviews are typically conducted by HR staff, and second interviews by the person who will be your line manager, in which case the interview may focus around whether you would fit into the team. Interviewers may be senior members of staff who may not be trained interviewers and may ask less orthodox questions.

How do they differ from first interviews?

Second interviews are similar to first interviews, with a few differences. The interview will be more closely related to the work you would do, and interviewers for technical roles may ask probing technical questions. It may be less formal, with reduced emphasis on competency questions but more testing overall. There might be questions on your cultural fit: how you will fit in with the ethos and values of the organization. You will find more about this in Chapter 3, 'Types of interview question'.

This interview might be the only component of the second stage, with perhaps a tour of the premises and a chance to meet recent graduate recruits. Many companies will, however, use an assessment centre in which the second interview will sit alongside tests, group exercises and presentations.

Second interviews are usually more demanding than first interviews, but occasionally not!

One candidate had a second interview with a manager who had supervised her placement. The interview lasted just 15 minutes and consisted mainly of questions about sailing, after which she was offered the post. She found out later that she had so impressed him on the placement that he had already decided to take her: the interview was merely a rubber-stamping exercise, and the questions about sailing were because he was going on a sailing holiday: he knew she was an excellent sailor and wanted some tips!

Another student, after impressing at the first interview, had a second interview with the cricket-mad senior partner of a local accountancy firm. The interview went something like this:

> **Partner:** 'I see you play cricket. Any good?'
>
> **Student:** 'I enjoy it a lot. I'm opening bowler for my local club and took quite a few wickets last season.'
>
> **Partner:** 'We're lacking a decent bowler for the firm's team – when can you start?'

How can I prepare?

Approach it like the first interview. Sell your strengths. Reread your research on the company and the job, and improve your answers to any questions you struggled to answer as these may come up again. Your first interviewer will have left notes on any perceived weaknesses or lack of knowledge or motivation, and so questions may focus around these.

Finding out more

On the Web

- **Group Interviews** University of Kent www.kent.ac.uk/careers/sk/teamwork.htm

Further reading

- See the book in this series: K Houston and E Cunningham, *How to Succeed at Assessment Centres* (Palgrave Study Skills, paperback, 2015).

Interviews for different roles

What you will learn in this chapter

- The types of interviews for different roles and how they differ
- How interviews for postgraduate study differ from interviews for jobs

Public sector interviews

These are typically highly structured competency interviews with most questions closely based on the job description, so have examples of evidence relating to the person specification ready. In the public sector, there are few spontaneous questions, and everything is asked with a purpose, as employers must demonstrate fairness and openness. Each candidate is asked identical questions, so these interviews are less biased but can be rigid, making it hard to appreciate the interviewee's personality.

A strong emphasis is placed on equal opportunities, with questions on how you would treat someone of a different race, religion, sex or disability, so give no suggestion of prejudice when answering. Show you understand the importance of everyone getting the same opportunities. One way is to give examples of discrimination that you, family members or friends have faced. Customer service organizations and those with a high public profile, such as the BBC and charities also use equal opportunity questions. They are common in interviews for the police, where examples of prejudice have thrown a spotlight on behaviour. There is a very good business case for policies of inclusivity as it maximizes the pool of potential candidates.

Sales and marketing interviews

Any interview is a marketing exercise: you are 'selling yourself' to the interviewer, and this is particularly so in this case. Say why you find the firm attractive, and find out about its products, services and competitors.

Mention experience you have in working to tight deadlines, working under pressure, meeting targets, getting the job done, being competitive and presenting to others. Mention examples you have of selling or promoting whilst at university. Perhaps you increased the membership of a society, sold lots of tickets for an event or were the publicity officer. You could also mention fundraising for a charity and customer service experience in shops and restaurants.

One company looked for 'helicopter ability' in marketing graduates: the ability to soar above a problem and to see all of its aspects rather than just the detail. Another important skill for marketing is multitasking – juggling a number of tasks at the same time. Sometimes you will be asked pressure questions such as in the following example. Don't take these personally – for these roles you must be able to withstand stress.

Sell me this pen!

A common question in marketing and sales interviews is, 'Sell me this pen', where the interviewer holds up a cheap pen, stapler or paper clip and asks you to 'sell' it to him or her.

Novice salespeople sell features: *'It has a cap, and the clip means you can store it upright, and it has a large store of ink so that it won't run out.'*

Experienced salespeople sell benefits: *'It's light and practical, and you can store it safely in your pocket. It doesn't matter if you lose it, as it's cheap, and it writes every time.'*

The best salespeople first establish the needs of the customer. Ask the interviewer questions to find out what their needs are, *'What kind of pens do you use?'*, *'What tasks do you use them for?'* to fit your approach to their requirements.

Computing interviews

If you are asked a technical question to which you don't know the answer, say you don't know and go on to say how you would find out.

Do you prefer the programming or analytical side of computing more?

In most companies, both technical and non-technical routes will be available. Answer honestly. The big consultancies will almost certainly have a route for programmers to progress and become the in-house 'guru' for a particular skill; but there may be more demand for those who start in programming and, after a year or two, move into analysis, project management and consultancy roles where they are less likely to be overtaken by technology changes as the basic skills of analysis remain the same whatever system you work on.

As a programmer, don't end up in a backwater – working in an outdated language but unable to work in other languages without training. Having said this, there is still a demand for programmers in legacy languages such as COBOL which are still used widely, on the basis of 'If it ain't broke, don't fix it.' Adverts which focus on particular languages may just want a coder and offer little chance for career development, whereas graduate training schemes in IT will be likely to offer you a variety of routes to progress. Ultimately, if you can answer this question by showing you are flexible and have skills on both sides, you are likely to be in high demand, especially if you have good communication and technical skills, as such people are hard to find.

What experience do you have of C# (or another programming language)?

New computing graduates are usually recruited more for their problem-solving skills than for knowledge of a particular language, so you can often answer this question by emphasizing your ability to learn; once you know one object-oriented language, you know that you can learn a new language in a few weeks.

Example answer for 'What experience do you have of C#'

It's true I don't know C#, but on my course I learned Java, which shares the same data types and control structures. There are few new concepts, and I'm confident I can rapidly learn to write efficient C# given some basic training. I'd love to learn C# as it's a fast-growing language which would add to my skill set, but more valuable to you are my problem-solving skills, which I can apply in any language.

Interviews for journalism and media jobs

These jobs are highly competitive to get and so you have to finely hone your interview skills. Show you have an interest in current affairs, people, places and events and can quickly build a rapport with people. Show evidence that you can cope with tight deadlines, can think on your feet and have a thick skin. Have questions to ask as the job is all about curiosity.

What makes a good journalist?

You must be able to work quickly and efficiently with the other staff as time is money. When there are tight deadlines, everyone has to pull together to get the job done. Interviewers will want to know that you can quickly establish a good rapport with people. You need good communication skills and a crisp, concise writing style: academic essays are NOT good evidence for this! They'll expect you to have a good knowledge of current affairs and a strong sense of curiosity, and to be flexible, especially with regard to working hours, so evidence of good time management skills, such as holding down part-time jobs whilst studying will help.

Increasingly, journalists have to work across formats; as well as writing an article, you might be taking photos and preparing content for the Web or recording an interview for broadcast, so you need to show good evidence of a mastery of the relevant (and fast-changing) technology.

How do you stay informed of the news?

Read a quality newspaper or news website daily to keep up to date with current affairs. Interviewers want to know what sources of news you use and whether you know the differences between them. A common question for TV journalism is about the difference between BBC and ITN news coverage, and for print journalism you might be asked the difference between the *Times* and the *Independent* for example. Don't be overtly political: you should aim to provide a balanced assessment of a topic of interest to you. Keep an eye on the different news media and the different ways they cover the news. What type of stories do they prioritize? Do they have a political affiliation? Who is their target audience? Do they have a particular style? How detailed is their coverage? Who covers the news most accurately?

Which recent news story would you have liked to cover?

Be honest: the story you choose doesn't matter. They want to see enthusiasm and real interest in the subject you choose, so choose a story that you know a lot about as you may get questioned about it. Show your awareness of a big story, the need for accuracy in reporting, what made it noteworthy, how it might be adapted to different media, what else you might have brought to it such as a different angle you might have taken and questions you would have asked.

What relevant experience do you have?

To get a job as a journalist you need to already have some practical journalism experience; usually, this is writing for the student newspaper. Occasionally, graduates have got into journalism by arguing brilliantly why they've never participated in student journalism, but this is rare. Increasingly, news organizations expect you to have a postgraduate qualification in journalism.

Create a portfolio of articles you've written. This may be just a few articles you have had published, as quality is more important than quantity. You need real news items as well as film reviews. Recent material, ideally from commercial publications, is valuable, but it doesn't need to be front-page stories. Recordings of university radio, TV broadcasts or web videos can help, but keep them short.

Interviews for placements and internships

Placement and internship interviews are usually a little easier than those for graduate roles. Companies take into account that placement students are typically younger and less experienced and also that the job is not permanent. The interview may include a tour of the premises. If so, ask questions about what you are being shown while you are being taken round to display interest. You may also get the chance to talk to current placement students.

Questions asked at placement and internship interviews

- If we were to offer you an internship, which area would you most like to work in?
- What do you want to achieve in your placement?
- Tell me about your project. (Talk about what you did, how you went about it, how you organized the project and, if it was a group project, how you split the work up between you.)
- Which part of your course do you like/dislike the most?
- When have you set yourself goals, and how did you reach them?
- Why did you apply to our company?
- What do you know about us? (If you've done careful research, as outlined in the first chapter of this book, you should be able to talk about the company's products and services, customers, competitors and what the company says makes them special.)

A student's experience

They gave us a questionnaire that asked about what we hoped to get out of the placement and what we liked about the company. I then had a tour and an interview where they only asked me about my favourite experiments at university and for an example of teamwork. I had to answer a maths question as well.

Interviews for casual jobs

Most students have to work during their degree to pay their way, and most casual student jobs in the vacations or in evenings and at weekends during term time are in shops, restaurants and offices. Interviewers will be looking less at your ability to write essays and pass exams than evidence of relevant practical skills, your enthusiasm to work hard and flexibility to do any task required, so only give brief details of your degree; you might, however, mention your English, maths and computing qualifications and perhaps language skills if you are working in a tourist town. Interviews may be quite short and informal: one student who had already worked in retail was only asked four questions in an interview for a temporary Christmas sales job, before being accepted.

If you can show you have useful skills and experience that can be put to good use from day one, you will be at an advantage. Give details of skills gained in other work that would be valuable in most jobs: prioritizing, administration, training and **customer service skills**.

Questions asked at interviews for casual jobs

- Describe a situation where you had to help others.
- Give me an example of where you have worked in a team? What was your role and contribution?
- How do you solve problems with people you don't like? (Many casual jobs involve serving people in customer service roles, so it's important that you can show tact with a customer, who is, for example, returning an item in a shop or complaining about cold food.)
- Have you ever missed any deadlines?
- Have you ever done something without having people to ask you to? (This checks whether you have initiative. If you've finished all of your allotted tasks, do you just stand about chatting, or do you look for other work that needs doing?)

Example answer to 'What skills can you bring to us?'

I have a capacity to work hard under pressure, and all my previous jobs have required me to work quickly and accurately and to show adaptability. My summer shop job involved working within a busy team and organization; co-ordination and commitment were needed to ensure daily sales targets were met. I built strong positive relationships with both customers and staff and provided shoppers with high-quality customer care.

Interviews for teacher training

Teaching interviews tend to be quite relaxed. You may get a group interview where you would be asked to discuss a number of topics in a group of candidates (see the section on group interviews in Chapter 5, 'Types of interview'.) as this shows how you cope in situations similar to those you meet in teaching. You may get a written test where your spelling, handwriting and grammar will be under observation.

Talk about how you could make a difference to pupils' lives, so think about how you would motivate students. Read about current developments in teaching. How do you, yourself, learn best? Through classes, seminars, work or self-learning?

Give evidence of interest in the age range for which you have applied. Interviewers are looking for a personality that will work well in a classroom. They really value enthusiasm, so act keen. Link your answers to your school or life experience. Give evidence of your ability to relate to young people outside the formal school curriculum: sports coaching, helping in a youth club, designing sets for a school play, teaching someone to play a musical instrument or a foreign language, to use a computer or mentoring younger students.

What experience do you have in schools?

Sell your teaching experience. Many courses don't interview candidates who don't have some recent experience of working with children of the relevant age group, although you might get away without this in a shortage subject such as maths. Contact schools well in advance, and keep a log book of your experience.

Describe the school and talk about what interested you during your classroom experience. Did a particular teacher inspire you? What did you do? What insights did you gain? How was the classroom laid out? If a lesson did not work, how might you do it differently? What teaching styles were used? Was there effective use of technology (whiteboards, computers)? How did the teacher's personality affect his or her teaching style? How was bad behaviour managed? How did they help less able children? How did the teacher assess work and give feedback?

> **Example answer for 'What is the relevance of your psychology degree to primary teaching?'**
>
> *Although my psychology degree is not a National Curriculum subject, it is relevant to teaching as it's based upon scientific analysis. Maths, IT and child development are also core components of my degree. I've learnt that information is better memorized in young children when visual and tactile aides are used. Through my course I've learnt that information is best grasped when presented in a supportive environment and introduced in manageable steps. I also recognize that it's not only the academic development of children that is important in school, but also their social relationships.*
>
> *One of my modules involved organizing an event, so I decided to organize one for children. Having met the children, they knew who I was and what I was trying to do, and so they respected me more. I could then communicate on a different level, speaking to them firmly when necessary, but also explaining clearly in language they could understand, so they weren't confused about what was going on and enjoyed the event more. I managed to get one girl who never participated in PE lessons in school to join in.*

Interviews for postgraduate study

If you apply for a taught masters course, you may not be interviewed with the decision made purely on your application, grades and references, but PhD candidates will always be interviewed. If you are given an offer on the basis of your application, do visit the university to make sure you'll be happy there.

There are many similarities to job interviews, such as the need to prepare well, show enthusiasm and ask questions. Academic interviews are less formal than job interviews and more like a relaxed chat, but sometimes you might be grilled on your subject knowledge. You may just be asked questions as you are shown round the department. Interviews for vocational courses may be more formal than interviews for research. Academics may not be trained interviewers, so occasionally you might need to take the initiative. Keep your answers succinct and to the point – don't waffle.

Smart casual dress is fine, but business departments might expect more formal dress than art schools. For vocational courses such as teaching, you'll be expected to dress in the same way as for a job interview. Interviews for research will require less formal clothes, but if unsure, dress smartly.

How can I prepare?

Research the department carefully, and prepare questions to ask such as *'What have previous students gone on to do?'* and *'How often would I meet my supervisor?'* Find out about links with employers, teaching methods and practical experience gained on the course. Read your application again to anticipate questions that may be asked. Contact your potential course supervisor beforehand to ask what they are looking for.

Choose your academic referees carefully. Arrange a meeting to get their advice on postgraduate study, and brief them on your application. You'll normally need two academic referees. One could be your academic adviser or tutor, and the second, perhaps, your project supervisor.

Look round both campus and town before going home. Speak to current students, and look at notice boards to gauge the department. Talk to other postgraduates about their interviews. Budget for interview as you probably won't be reimbursed. Occasionally, you might get a group interview. See the section on group interviews in Chapter 5, 'Types of interview'.

Interviews for research

Find out who funds the research by the group, who works in the department and what their research interests are. Read papers published by your potential supervisor and other group members. What techniques do they use? What kind of students does the university have? It's fine to get in touch with relevant staff to talk about your research proposal. Find out what your potential supervisor is like as a person by talking to current research students.

Have ideas about what you want to research and how you would tackle it, how it excites you and why. What will be the impact of your research? Your research proposal doesn't need to be perfect; it's fine if it's a little rough round the edges, but competition will be greater if the research is funded.

Some members of the interview panel may not be specialists in your subject, so be able to explain your research without too much jargon. Practise explaining it to friends and family.

Interviewers will want to find out about you as a person. How will you manage working alone for much of the time? Will you fit in to the team? This is especially important in smaller departments. Show your commitment to further learning, as this is the ultimate transferable skill. Interviewers will be looking for tenacity, problem-solving skills and lateral thinking. Know your strengths: project management or picking the salient points from a research publication. If you know any technical skills you might use in the PhD, do emphasize these.

Questions you might be asked

Why do you want to study here?

Don't say you want to go to the university because it's esteemed and prestigious: academics hate empty praise. Talk instead about specific areas of research or specialisms and how these match your own interests; different methods of teaching; links with industry and your first-degree modules. Be open about applications to other universities as they'll expect you to have reserve choices.

Example answer for 'Why do you want to study here?'

I want to study at a university in or around London with a strong record of research in the field I wish to enter. I like the structure of the course, with its emphasis on practical learning and flexibility in choice of modules. Your strong links with industry and good employment record are also important to me for my future career plans. Your module on the impact of globalization on businesses particularly attracts me as I've studied this as part of my degree and would like to undertake my dissertation on this.

What skills do you have?

Interviewers will be looking at your ability to think for yourself – your capacity for independent and original thought, to communicate and to reason. Be ready to argue and to state your opinions rather than giving the answer that you think they want, as they'll be looking more at your ideas, attitudes and opinions than getting the 'right answer'. Give examples of relevant skills from both academic and non-academic contexts; for example you might have learned how to manage your time by holding down a part-time job whilst studying.

Be honest about areas that you need to improve, as you don't need to be expert on everything. Just say that you are prepared to work hard on any areas in which you are weak. Can you cope with a high workload? Give examples of where you have shown resilience and determination, as these are important for postgraduate study.

What do you want to do after you've finished?

The interviewer will want to know what you expect to do after the course. Show you have a clear career goal and how the course will help you to achieve this, as you will be more committed to your study and less likely to give up. The interviewer will consider whether the course will help you achieve your goals, but won't expect an answer cast in stone – just an idea of where the course might lead you, whether this be teaching, research, consultancy or work in industry.

What is the relevance of your first degree?

Talk about how your degree has prepared you for postgraduate study. Have you studied relevant modules? Completed a relevant project or dissertation? What knowledge do you have? Do you read around the subject? They will look for evidence of passion for the subject. Do you genuinely seem to enjoy talking about it, and do you keep up to date with recent developments? Don't be boring.

Tell me about any projects or dissertations you've done?

Interviewers will want to know about your project or dissertation, as this may be the closest thing you've done to real research. They'll want to know how you chose it, how you undertook it, what you got out of it and what you enjoyed, so read your project submission again. They might ask you to justify the results. If it was a group project, they will be interested in what role you took in the team and how you co-operated with the other members, especially when problems arose. If it was an individual project, talk about the discipline of having to work independently with little supervision, having to find things out for yourself and how you went about solving problems. If you used any techniques that you may be using in your postgraduate study, then emphasize these. You could bring a copy of your project report, but the interviewer will be more interested in what you say.

Have you any questions?

Ask questions in the interview to show interest:

- What is special about this particular course/department?
- What are your requirements for this course/research?
- What are the tutorial/supervisory arrangements?
- What is the likelihood of financial support, and where will it come from?
- Am I a suitable candidate for nomination for an award?
- Who has sponsored previous students?
- What are the destinations/employment prospects of previous students?

Research interviewees could also ask if they could expect to earn extra money by taking seminars, invigilating, and so on.

You will find help with answering other postgraduate study interview questions on the companion website.

Finding out more

On the companion website www.palgravecareerskills.com

- Example answers and answer tips to more questions for different roles

On the Web

- **Interviews for teaching** Times Educational Supplement www.tes.co.uk
- **How to create a portfolio** University of Kent www.kent.ac.uk/ careers/cv/portfolios.htm

Telephone, Skype and video interviews

What you will learn in this chapter

- The difference between face-to-face interviews and telephone interviews
- Why companies are increasingly using telephone interviews
- Advantages and disadvantages of the telephone interview
- Techniques to help you perform well in a telephone interview
- About Skype, video and robotic interviews

> *The telephone is such an important invention that one day every town will have one.*
>
> Alexander Graham Bell

Telephone interviews

A telephone interview will usually be given to candidates who have passed the application stage. It is often a sifting interview to cut down a large number of applicants to shortlist for a face-to-face interview.

Why are they used?

Telephone interviews are increasingly used by employers as a first stage interview for many jobs – more than half of all large companies now use them. This is because they are very cost-effective as no travel costs need be paid by either party, and they are easy to arrange and quick to carry out. You don't need to arrange an interview room or look after the candidate. Increasingly for graduate training schemes, the next stage after a telephone interview is an assessment centre, with no face-to-face interview in between, although you would then get a face-to-face interview as part of the assessment centre.

What are their advantages and disadvantages?

The advantage for you is that they save you time and money: you don't need to travel to interview or dress up or even dress at all. One student said she had conducted the interview in her pyjamas. You also have the advantage that you can refer to your CV or application form and notes on how to answer likely questions.

The big negative is that you can't see the interviewer to gauge his or her body language, so you must listen carefully for verbal clues. If the employer is calling you, the interviewer will probably give you an approximate time he or she will call you – morning or afternoon on a given day. Such interviews can also go very quickly – as mentioned, they are usually shorter than face-to-face interviews. Thus, you have less time to think about your answers – so be well prepared!

How long do telephone interviews last?

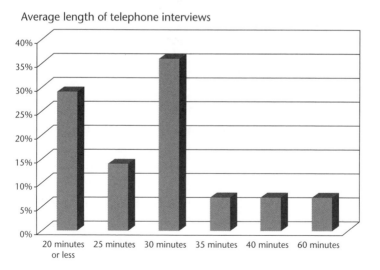

Average length of telephone interviews

Based on a sample of students who have had telephone interviews, the average length was half an hour, and they varied in length from 20 minutes to 1 hour.

Who uses telephone interviews?

Telephone interviews are particularly common for sales jobs, recruitment consultancy and, obviously, telesales. They test your verbal communication skills and phone skills, so they are appropriate for any job where you might need to spend a lot of time on the phone (for example public relations). Big companies use them more often than do smaller organizations.

Telephone interviews are also often used if you are applying for a job abroad – much cheaper than flying you hundreds of miles. You can use this to your advantage. If you are applying to a job a long way from where you live, you could suggest to the employer that he or she conduct an initial telephone interview or, even better, a Skype interview using a webcam, thus saving the time and expense of a face-to-face interview.

Will the questions be different?

No, they will be identical to those you would get in a normal interview. Here are some questions that students have been asked at telephone interviews.

- How did you choose your university?
- Why do you want to work for us?
- When have you used your initiative to achieve a goal?
- Tell me about a time when you had to persuade someone to change his or her mind and how you achieved this?
- What qualities are important to work in the role you are applying for?
- What evidence can you give to show you possess these qualities?
- What do we do?
- Describe a situation when you have exceeded a customer's expectations.
- Give an example of when you had to deal with a difficult customer.

Tips from an employer

Make sure you answer the question! It sounds really simple and obvious, but so often when asked a long, competency-based question, candidates start explaining a situation but don't clearly answer the question. Keep the question clearly in your mind, and keep referring back to it while you answer. Don't be afraid to note it down, using pen and paper, or ask the interviewer to repeat – an interview isn't a memory test.

John Lewis Partnership

Will there be anything else to do?

Normally, you will just get an interview, but sometimes you may get situational judgement questions where a situation is described and you are asked what course of action you would take. (See Chapter 3, 'Types of interview question', for more about this type of question.) If you are given tests, these are much more likely to be personality tests involving multiple choice or true/false answers rather than numerical and verbal aptitude tests.

Your voice

Your voice assumes much more importance in a telephone interview than in a face-to-face interview, where interviewers can also judge you on your body language, so it's important to make the most of your voice.

Vary the pace of your delivery a little to add colour, and pause occasionally. Also vary the pitch (how high or deep your voice sounds), the volume (louder and softer) and the tone. Stress certain important words, and leave short pauses occasionally. Take a little time before answering questions, rather than blurting them out immediately, as this can make you sound more confident and assertive.

Speaking slowly and with a slightly deeper voice than you normally use will make you sound more confident and self-possessed. Slowing your speech also gives you more time to think and improves the impact of what you say, but don't speak too slowly or you may sound boring. Breathing deeply will also help you to relax.

A study[1] found that voters in elections are more likely to pick candidates with a deeper voice. Researchers also found that women with lower voices were viewed as stronger, more trustworthy and competent. People who speak with a lower pitch can convey dominance, whereas people who speak with higher frequencies may be perceived as more kindly and submissive.

> *Margaret Thatcher took voice-coaching lessons before she became Prime Minister, to lower the pitch of her voice.*

Researchers at Glasgow University[2] found that people take under a second to form an impression of someone's personality based on just their voice. Voices transmit information about our gender, age, strength and personality. Researchers extracted the single word 'hello' from recordings by different people and asked 320 listeners to rate this for personality traits including trustworthiness, dominance and attractiveness. Listeners agreed closely to the extent each voice represented each trait. The pitch of the voice influenced how trustworthy the person seemed: a man who raises his pitch becomes more trustworthy, whereas a girl who glides from a high to a low pitch is seen as more trustworthy than one whose pitch rises at the end of the word.

Newsreaders lower their pitch at the end of phrases, as this sounds more authoritative. For example, if you say '*Can I speak to the HR manager please?*', if you lower your pitch on *please* instead of raising it, you sound more authoritative.

Simplify your words: Research by Daniel Oppenheimer[3] found that the use of overly complex words makes people sound less intelligent and can put off interviewers. He found that using simpler language led to a perception of higher intelligence, whereas the use of difficult language without good reason made the person seem less intelligent. So you can be perceived as more intelligent by simplifying your language.

> *Simplicity is the ultimate sophistication.*
>
> Leonardo da Vinci

Tips

- If you are asked to phone the company, this gives you control over the time of the interview but you'll have to pay for the call.
- Keep in front of you a list of the key selling points you wish to make, the job description and a list of questions you wish to ask, plus bulleted answers to questions.
- If you don't know when the employer will phone, keep your CV or application form, notes on the job and your answers to questions near to your phone. If the call does come unexpectedly and you are not prepared, say, '*Thank you for calling. Do you mind waiting for a minute while I close the door?*' This will give you time to compose yourself. If it really is a bad time, offer to call back at an agreed time.
- If you have a hands-free phone it will be easier to make notes.

> *One student had a fire alarm go off in the middle of her telephone interview!*

- Use a private room and close the door to reduce background noise. Put 'Do Not Disturb' on the door.
- Smile when you dial! Smiling when you speak really does make a difference to your tone of voice.
- Note down the name of your interviewer.
- If you prefer standing up when the interview is in progress, adopt a power pose such as standing tall, puffing your chest out and stretching yourself out, or even putting your feet on the desk (see Chapter 2, 'First impressions', for more about power posing). This will increase your testosterone, making you feel more confident. Standing up will also increase the power of your voice: ask any singer! Sitting up straight will make you feel more professional.
- When answering questions, don't just read out the notes you have made as this will sound stilted.
- Listen carefully to the interviewer and try to answer with a lively tone of voice. The call centre where the interviewer is based might be noisy, so speak clearly, reasonably loudly and not too quickly.
- When talking face-to-face, you show that you are listening via non-verbal signals such as nodding your head, but over the phone

you have to show this by the occasional 'okay', 'uh-huh', 'I see', 'I understand' and 'yes'. However, you can't keep saying 'uh-huh' for too long without sounding false, so reflect back what the speaker is saying, using other words. This shows you're listening carefully and trying to understand. It's the most useful way of giving positive feedback to someone: 'I hear what you're saying and take you seriously'.

- Immediately after the interview, write down the questions you were asked and any ways in which you could have improved your responses.

Tips from an employer

As the interviewer can't see you use this to your advantage. Dress comfortably or smartly if this makes you feel confident, spread notes around the table or on the walls as prompts. Don't be afraid to ask the interviewer to phone you back on a landline or mobile if you think the reception would be clearer.

John Lewis Partnership

Preparation checklist for a telephone interview

❏ Have you checked your answerphone message in case you miss a call? Does it give a professional impression?

❏ Have you found a quiet location where you won't be disturbed?

❏ Have you told the other people in the building that you are having an interview and not to disturb you?

❏ If the company will be phoning you on a landline have you told other people in the house to let you answer?

❏ Have you got a desk where you can make notes with a pen, notepad and glass of water on it?

❏ Is your phone charged, switched on, in credit and with a good signal? Is it easily accessible so that you can get to it quickly when it rings?

❏ Is your laptop turned on if you have notes or information on it?

❏ Have you got a copy of your application and information on the company plus notes on how to answer likely questions in front of you?

❏ Have you prepared a list of your unique selling points (USPs) to put across? See Chapter 1, 'Preparing for the interview', for more about USPs.

Skype interviews

Conducting interviews via Skype offers employers all the advantages of a telephone interview, with the bonus of being able to see the candidate. The ability to see the interviewer allows the interview to feel more natural as you can pick up non-verbal signals such as head nodding.

Skype interviews aren't as widely used as telephone interviews, but they are very helpful when applying for jobs abroad, where getting to a traditional interview would be expensive and time-consuming. Universities often use them when interviewing candidates for postgraduate study and research, and they are becoming increasingly popular.

A Skype interview will be more similar to a face-to-face interview than a telephone interview, but bear in mind the following:

❏ Make sure that you are suitably dressed as this will make you feel confident. You could, however, wear your pyjama bottoms if these are out of view! Make sure that the background looks tidy.
❏ Look into the webcam so that you are talking directly to the employer – and smile! Make sure the webcam views your face and shoulders. Sit up straight rather than slouching.
❏ Speak clearly into the microphone. Don't speak at the same time as the interviewer as this can make it difficult to hear what is being said on Skype.
❏ Choose a sensible Skype name: foxy.sally may not impress employers!

> *One student was interviewed in the UK from California for a place on the BUNAC Work America programme. The interviewer could see the garden in the background through the window and started the interview by asking what the weather was like in England.*

Additional checklist for a Skype interview

❏ Have you dressed as smartly as you would for a normal interview?
❏ Have you checked that the interviewer won't be distracted by tatty posters or your unmade bed in the background?

❏ If you live on the ground floor, consider drawing the curtains to avoid 'friends' pulling faces through the window, but make sure that the lighting is bright so the interviewer can see you clearly.

❏ Have you asked a friend to Skype you before the interview, to check that everything is working, the background is clear and your notes are out of view?

❏ Have you turned off other programs running on your computer: if you have an old computer, this could slow down the connection, and you also don't want to be distracted by an email popping up while you are speaking.

❏ If your broadband is slow, have you asked other people in the house to stop downloading, so the connection doesn't lag at a crucial time?

❏ Have you got the phone number or email for your interviewer so that you can contact him or her if there are any technical problems?

❏ Have you turned off your mobile and taken landline phones off the hook?

❏ Consider attaching brief notes to the side of your screen so you don't need to look down to refer to these, thus maintaining good eye contact with the interviewer.

Video interviews

The use of recorded video interviews started with technology companies but has now spread to mainstream employers. Large graduate recruiters such as John Lewis, Grant Thornton, CERN, AXA, PWC, Volvo and BT are increasingly turning to video interviewing or viewing video CVs. Video interviews are different from phone or Skype interviews in that there is no interviewer present, and interviewees are presented with pre-recorded questions. A video interview is as 'real' as an interview in an office and can be better than a phone interview as it can be reviewed and marked at any time, greatly speeding up the process.

Video interviews normally take place after you have submitted your application form and online tests, and before you are invited to a face-to-face interview or assessment centre.

Advantages of video interviews

- Interviewers can review your interview at any time or place, making much more efficient use of their time, and they can be much cheaper than face-to-face interviews.
- They can replay and rate the interviews online, so they can compare candidates without having to remember who said what and can also review anything of particular interest. They can also share interviews with colleagues to get a second opinion.
- Video interviews are good for rating the interviewee's impact, presentability, confidence, personality, verbal fluency, cultural fit and attitude.
- All interviewees get asked the same questions in exactly the same way, reducing the chance of bias.
- Interviewees can schedule the interview at their own convenience, without having to travel or take time off from work or study.
- Interviewees can normally try a practice interview before their real interview begins.

> In one video interview, the interviewee's cat jumped onto the table right in front of the camera and refused to move.

Disadvantages of video interviews

- Some candidates have found the experience uncomfortable.
- The interviewer can't probe interviewees on their answers.
- You get none of the feedback you'd expect from an interview with a real interviewer.

A typical structure for the video interview

- You schedule the interview via the employer's website. Students are sent an invite from the recruiting company via a specialist interview video company such as Sonru, LaunchPad or InterviewStream.
- You can complete the video interview on your PC or by downloading an app for your smartphone or tablet. A tutorial provides tips on how to use the webcam and on the interview itself, and a test assesses the sound and vision quality of your computer or phone.

> According to a survey by the video interview company Sonru,[4] 74 per cent of their candidates conducted interviews via the Web, and 26 per cent via Apple or Android. Eighty-six per cent of the video interviews were conducted at home, and over half at the weekend.

- You get a chance to practise using the software with some random practice questions. You can practise as many times as you wish, and you can watch your practice video to help you to improve your performance.
- Once you start the real interview, you are given a series of questions. Like a traditional interview, you don't see the questions in advance and respond to one question at a time. You have 30 to 60 seconds to read each question and prepare your answer before the recording starts. You then have about two minutes to record each answer. If you finish your answer before the time is up, you can click to go to the next question. Once you click to start the interview, there is no turning back as you aren't allowed to rerecord it or rewind or review your answers.

Exercise: Answer an interview question on video

Using your phone or computer, record on video your answer to the following question, taking no more than two minutes.

Describe a time when you succeeded at a difficult challenge.

Once you have finished, play back your answer. Did you look professional? How did your voice sound? Show your video to a friend to get some feedback.

Was your answer well structured? Interviewers ask this question to see if you have resilience and determination: do you keep going when the going gets tough, or give up? Do you stay positive under pressure? Can you overcome difficulties and find creative solutions to problems? See Chapter 4, 'How to STAR at competency questions', for further help on how to answer.

How to prepare

Many of the tips given above for Skype interviews also apply.

❏ Make sure that the lighting is good in the room (draw the curtains if you need to) and that your background looks simple and tidy, and move the camera if necessary.

❏ Practise using your webcam: record yourself to see how you appear on camera to check that your image is clear and bright. Dress smartly as you would for a face-to-face interview, and make sure your shirt or blouse contrasts with the background. Keep the camera at eye level. Get close enough to the camera so that your head and shoulders are in clear view and look directly into the camera, not at your image on the screen, as you will then be more engaging.

❏ Follow the directions carefully, and don't be put off by the timer counting down.

❏ Speak loudly and clearly, and smile!

❏ It's easy to have either too much or too little to say, and not use the time properly, so prepare carefully for the interview and practise giving answers within two minutes.

❏ Ask for help (available online or by phone) if you don't know how the webcam works or if you have any questions.

Tips from an employer

This isn't a live interview – it's a video that you record for us. We'll provide you with a log-in to the system, where you can read questions our interviewers have prepared for you. You then use a webcam and microphone to record a video of you answering these questions, and it is automatically uploaded for us to watch. The system is designed to walk you through each stage so it is simple to do and time efficient for everyone.

Ensure you are in a controlled environment where you will not be disturbed by phones ringing, someone knocking on the door, dogs barking, etc., etc.!

John Lewis Partnership

Robot interviews

Some organizations are now using virtual interviewers via online video interview software. Life-like avatars ask the questions normally asked by an interviewer. The avatar is visible during the whole interview so that the interviewee has something to focus on and keeps them engaged by using visual, audio and text prompts. Avatars increase consistency by asking each question in exactly the same way to each interviewee.

Hello Anne Droid, I'm Rob, your interviewer!

Virtual interviews save organizations money by greatly reducing the time involved in the process and can improve the candidate's interview experience. One American company called Starfighter has taken the ultimate step. It has designed a game which involves hacking into Government software (not the real systems of course), and the players with the most talent are offered jobs.

Finding out more

On the Web

Video Interview companies
- **Sonru** www.sonru.com
- **LaunchPad** www.launchpadrecruits.com
- **Interviewstream** http://interviewstream.com

References

1 C Klofstad, R Anderson and S Peters, 'Sounds like a Winner: Voice Pitch Influences Perception of Leadership Capacity' (2012), Royal Society of London B. doi/10.1098/rspb.2012.0311.

2 P McAleer, A Todorov and P Belin, 'How Do You Say "Hello"? Personality Impressions from Brief Novel Voices' (2014), PLoS ONE 9(3): e90779. doi:10.1371/journal.pone.0090779.

3   DM Oppenheimer, 'Consequences of Erudite Vernacular Utilized Irrespective of Necessity: Problems with Using Long Words Needlessly' (2014), *Applied Cognitive Psychology*, 20, 139–56. doi: 10.1002/acp.1178.
4   Sonru. Report on 200,000 Insights on the Candidate Experience of Video Interviewing www.sonru.com/images/uploads/ Summary_Insights_2_Page.pdf

Chapter 8

The end of the interview and afterwards

Contents

- The end of the interview
- After the interview
- If you get an offer
- If you are rejected
- Action planning

What you will learn in this chapter

- What to do at the end of the interview and afterwards
- What to do if you get an offer
- How to keep your spirits up if rejected
- The importance of action planning
- Resources to take you even further

The end of the interview

When you are asked if you have any questions, it's a sign that the interview is drawing to its close. Ask intelligent questions; this was covered in Chapter 1, 'Preparing for the interview'.

Check the next steps. If it hasn't already been made clear, ask whether this is the only interview and, if not, what the next stage would be and when you will hear the decision.

Last impressions linger! After the start of the interview, the end is the part interviewers most remember, so be enthusiastic. Smile, shake hands firmly and say how much you enjoyed the meeting. Try to address the interviewer by name: *'I'd like to say how much I've enjoyed this interview Ms Kowalski, and I really like what I've heard about the company.'* Don't, of course, ask how you've done.

> *At the end of his interview, one interviewee shook the interviewer's hand, opened the (wrong) door and walked confidently into a wardrobe.*

It's unlikely that you'll be offered a job on the spot, but if you are, and are unsure about the job, avoid accepting immediately. Say how delighted you are to be offered it, and ask for a short time to consider.

After the interview

Immediately after the interview, while your memory is clear, write down anything important that the interviewer told you, such as his or her name and job title, when you'll hear the result, the next steps in the process, the questions you were asked and those you feel you gave a poor answer to, so you can work out a better response in the future. Take a small notepad and pen with you, or use your smartphone for this.

The thank-you note

The day after the interview, write a short thank-you email to the interviewer, and mention specific points from the interview. Few people do this, but as well as being good manners, it may just make a difference or lead to future opportunities. An interviewer may interview 15 people for a job but will only remember a few of these. Instead of sending an email, consider writing a letter. Most managers get hundreds of emails every day but rarely get letters.

Example thank-you note

Thank you for taking the time to see me yesterday. I greatly enjoyed meeting you and having the opportunity to hear about the company and your training scheme. I am enthusiastic about the role and the challenges and prospects open to me should I be successful. I feel that my potential would make me an asset to your team, and I would be greatly pleased were I to be offered the post.

If you get an offer

Congratulations! Ask for a letter to confirm the details in writing outlining the terms of your employment. Verbal offers can be withdrawn, whereas written offers are normally legally binding. This will also prevent misunderstandings later.

If you are a strong candidate, you may get several offers, and if you are unsure whether to accept your first offer, email the employer, thanking the company for the offer and stating when you'll be able to confirm your decision. Companies will be used to students asking for time to decide and will view this more favourably than if you accept and then withdraw later. Not all companies will give you more time, in which case you'll need to make a decision.

If the employer has given a deadline for you to confirm, try to get this extended. If you have only the one offer and no interviews coming up, it might be wise to accept. If you have more interviews lined up, you could take a risk.

If you've received an offer and want to ask other organizations to which you've applied about the progress of your application, you can try to persuade your first-choice employer to hurry up with a decision. Contact your first-choice employer to ask when you'll hear the outcome, letting the company know that it is your preferred choice: 'I'm really keen to work for you, but I've been offered another job. How soon could you let me know if I've been successful?' If the company really wants you, the people in charge of hiring might speed up their decision.

Negotiating the salary

In the private sector, you might be able to negotiate your salary if you are unhappy with it, whereas in the public sector the salary is usually set. If asked to name a figure, set this higher rather than lower as they won't withdraw an offer simply because you value your worth. If you have done your research using sites such as Glassdoor.co.uk, you should know the going rate for the job.

Having said this, initial salary should matter less than opportunities for training and career development. If the salary will increase greatly in a year or two, don't worry if the starting salary isn't high; job satisfaction, good colleagues, prospects for advancement and a supportive work environment matter more than earning another thousand pounds.

If you are rejected

Don't let rejection get you down; don't blame yourself as this will reduce your confidence. Avoid negative self-talk such as 'I'm a failure', and convert it into something positive: 'I've learned a lot.' There is no real failure, only learning and improving.

Console yourself with the thought that at least you were selected for interview. Fewer than one in five applicants are typically interviewed, so you were probably in the top 20 per cent. Take an evening off, and let your hair down. Forget about job-hunting so that you start again refreshed.

Many organizations don't notify candidates that they've been rejected, so if you haven't heard anything within a week of your interview, email to find out how you stand.

Consider also applying for less competitive jobs. For example, there is much competition for graduate jobs in marketing but less for the fast-growing areas of digital marketing and corporate sales, so it's easier to get interviews for these. Moreover, these can be pathways into standard marketing.

Get feedback on your performance

If you are rejected, try phoning the interviewer while his or her memory is fresh to politely ask why you were unsuccessful. If you get no response, then try emailing instead. Politely explain that feedback would help greatly to improve your interview skills. Many interviewers won't give negative feedback and will simply say you were a strong candidate but that the successful candidate was slightly better.

Ask questions such as these:

- Were there any questions I didn't answer well?
- How could I have made a better impression?
- What did the successful candidate do better than I did?

If you don't get any offers after several interviews, set up a mock interview with your careers adviser as this may quickly pinpoint any major flaws.

Learn from each interview

Learn from each interview, and you will improve and eventually get a good offer. I find that once a candidate has been invited to one interview, he or she often gets invited to others in quick succession, having 'cracked' the application stage; for such people, their applications are now of such a quality that they are perceived as an attractive candidate.

Exercise: Analyse your performance

Were there any gaps in the research you carried out on the company, job or industry?

How well did you answer the interviewer's questions?

Write below any you answered poorly, and work on an improved answer for next time.

Did you put the interviewer at ease?

Could you improve on the questions you asked?

Don't let it get you down

> When one door closes, another opens; but we often look so long and so regretfully upon the closed door that we do not see the one which has opened for us.
>
> Alexander Graham Bell

Job-hunting involves a lot of rejection and may sap the confidence of even the best applicants. Try not to take this rejection personally as you can't get every job you go for. Perhaps there was one outstanding applicant with a little more experience than you who got the job. It isn't the end of the world; there will be other jobs you can apply for. Try instead to see it as an experience to be learned from. To be successful, you must learn how to cope with rejection and not to take it personally.

No

No

No

No

No

No

No

No

No

YES!

Getting a job is a series of nos followed by a single yes, but you only need the one yes: a job offer.

Don't just make one application at a time. If you have a number of applications in the pipeline at any one time, you may have other interviews to look forward to, and this will make a rejection less hard. If you have just one interview in the pipeline, it can make you more anxious because you will feel that everything depends on it.

The value of failure

If I find 10,000 ways something won't work, I haven't failed. I am not discouraged, because every wrong attempt discarded is another step forward.

Thomas Alva Edison

Being resilient involves reacting positively to negative outcomes. Learning to cope with adversity helps to make you stronger by teaching you how to bounce back. The most successful people are often those who've had the most failures, as they tend to be more adventurous. When things are not going right, they display tenacity, taking a positive attitude towards frustration and failure.

> *There is an old saying: 'A calm sea never made for a skilful sailor.' In other words, we only grow when we face challenges.*

When something goes wrong such as being rejected at interview, we tend to worry, magnify things out of proportion and become stressed. However, if we step back, we find that these can be times of growth. They force us to look at life through fresh eyes and reassess where we are heading. When we have problems, we become stronger in facing these and more sympathetic to problems faced by others. We learn new ways of coping and develop in new directions.

Without change, life becomes flat, predictable and boring. Without difficulties, you stay shallow, superficial and don't develop the maturity to face problems. When problems occur, take the energy you put into worrying and instead channel it into finding innovative solutions.

> *If we had no winter, the spring would not be so pleasant: if we did not sometimes taste adversity, prosperity would not be so welcome.*
>
> Anne Bradstreet

The best way to learn is from your mistakes, as once you've made a serious error, you are unlikely to repeat it. If you've never failed, you've never taken a risk. Failures should be thought of as opportunities for learning as you learn far more from failures than from successes.

High performers accept feedback non-defensively. Sometimes you'll make mistakes or do things in ways that could be improved. Positive performers understand that criticism in these situations isn't personal; it helps them perform better.

> *The man who never makes a mistake is the man who never does anything.*
>
> President Theodore Roosevelt

Action planning

I sometimes see graduates who completed their degree a year before and are now working long hours in a restaurant or bar. After a hard day's work, they don't have the time or energy to think about their future and consequently get stuck in a rut. The solution is to develop a plan to reach your goals. Action planning helps you to focus your ideas and to decide what steps to take to achieve your goals. An action plan can help you to reach goals in all aspects of your life, including interviews. Don't worry about the future – start planning for it instead.

When you take steps towards a goal, it activates the reward system in your brain, causing the release of a neurotransmitter called dopamine, which makes you feel good. You want to repeat the actions you made to feel this way, and so working towards your goal becomes pleasurable and keeps you motivated.

> *A goal without a plan is just a wish.*
>
> Antoine de Saint-Exupéry

Action planning involves:

- Identifying your objectives.
- Setting objectives which are achievable and measurable.

- Identifying the steps needed to achieve your goals.
- Prioritizing your tasks.
- Having a contingency plan.

Write down your plan

A study of job seekers by Professor Daniel Turban[1] found that writing a plan at the start of a job search has a big impact on success. Thinking about a plan, acting on a plan and reflecting upon that plan were important. If you write down your commitments, you tend to live up to these, as written commitments require more effort to make than verbal ones and also act as a reminder. The process of writing things down seems to embed the commitment in your brain. When you reach your goal, set another and write that one down too, and you'll be up and away.

> 'A goal properly set is halfway reached.'
>
> Abraham Lincoln

Exercise: Decide your goal or objective

This must be **SMART**.

S	**Specific:** *clear and unambiguous.*
M	**Measurable:** *How will you know you've reached your goal?*
A	**Achievable:** *Your aim must be realistic and not a pipe dream like 'One day I'll be a rock star!'*
R	**Relevant:** *It must have real importance to you.*
T	**Time Bound:** *You need a clear date when you expect to have reached your goal.*

Write your objective here. *(For example: to improve my interview skills, get a marketing internship, to increase my confidence)*

When will I start? *(For example after my exams)*

By when do I hope to have reached my goal? (For example in six months' time, in June next year)

Whom can you tell your plan to?

Tell friends or relatives about your goals to provide support when the going gets tough and to give you an incentive to keep going: you'll feel embarrassed to tell them you've given up. Public commitment makes you more determined, so also write about your goal on Facebook, Twitter or even a blog. Mix with positive people who will encourage you to keep going.

- *Family Members:*
- *Friends:*
- *Others (university staff, teachers):*

Decide the steps you will need to take

Goals are like recipes; you take one step at a time. Segmenting your goals will help you stay calm and focused on the process. Think of all the things you could do to take you closer to achieving your goal, no matter how small. Break down large steps into smaller components, so they seem easier to achieve.

First, brainstorm your ideas on a blank sheet of paper, or use a mind map. A mind map is a diagram to visually organize information. The subject of the map is in the centre of a blank page. Ideas in words or pictures branch out from the central subject. See the end of this chapter for mind map links.

Don't worry about the order. Write down as many steps as you can think of, even if they seem insignificant or unlikely to work. Don't criticize your ideas at this stage – just keep writing things down to keep the flow going. Once you've run out of ideas, go through your list and remove irrelevant items.

Next, define clearly the above steps. Be detailed and specific (not 'I'll practise interviews', but 'I'll arrange for my friend to give me a mock interview next weekend'. For example:

- I will research the employer, job and industry sector.
- I will make a list of my unique selling points.
- I will prepare a list of questions to ask.

Exercise: Putting the steps in order

Arrange the steps into chronological order with a date to start each step, and put these in your calendar. Set weekly goals: get into the habit of timetabling your tasks for the next week.

Build in rewards: Think of rewards for completing each step, to keep motivated. The bigger the step, the larger the reward.

- STEP 1: *Some nice chocolate*
- STEP 2: *More chocolate!*
- STEP 3: *Time in gym to burn off chocolate*

List the steps you need to take. Be detailed and specific.	My reward	Date to start this step
Step 1		
Step 2		
Step 3 (add further steps as required)		

What problems might I face? How will I overcome these?

We tend to underestimate how long projects will take, as we expect everything to go to plan. Invariably, things go wrong, so consider what you would do if you failed to reach your goals. Build flexibility into your plan by mapping several paths. Then if one becomes blocked, another is available.

What barriers might prevent me achieving my goal?

List any problems you might encounter. What could you do to overcome these problems? *(For example 'I get very nervous at interviews, so I'll learn mindfulness techniques to reduce this.')*

Keep reviewing your progress

Turn every problem into a challenge and every challenge into an opportunity. Keep a diary of your activities, and record your progress, as this keeps your plan concrete. A good time to start your review is two weeks after you've begun. Review how far you've got towards your objective; identify any mistakes you've made and what you can learn from these. Consider any new opportunities that may have arisen, and incorporate these into your plan. Get into the habit of making lists of things you need to do, as these mini action plans will help you to organize your life effectively.

Finding out more

On the Web

- **Mind mapping** http://en.wikipedia.org/wiki/Mind_map
- **Coping with rejection** www.kent.ac.uk/careers/sk/ copingWithRejection.htm

Further reading

- S Rook, *The Graduate Career Guidebook: Advice for Students and Graduates on Careers Options, Jobs, Volunteering, Applications, Interviews and Self-employment* (Palgrave Study Skills, paperback, 2013).

References

1 DB Turban, CK Stevens and FK Lee, 'Effects of Conscientiousness and Extraversion on New Labor Market Entrants' Job Search: The Mediating Role of Meta-cognitive Activities and Positive Emotions' (2009) *Personnel Psychology*, 62, 553–73.

Try a practice interview

Contents

What will you learn in this chapter

- Try a practice interview by recording yourself answering common interview questions or with a friend asking you the questions and giving you feedback on your answers.
- Get tips on how to answer the questions.
- Use a report form of the type used by interviewers, to assess your performance.
- Gain confidence so you are calmer at the real interview.

Practising on your own

Think of a job that you are particularly keen on getting, and then ask yourself the following questions. Have a real job and employer in mind that you would like to work for when you answer the questions, as this will make it more realistic. Each time you have a practice interview, or a real one for that matter, your anxiety is likely to reduce a little due to a process called desensitization.

You can write your answers down on paper, but – even better – dictate them into a voice recorder so you can listen to how you would sound to an interviewer.

You could also use your webcam or practise in front of a mirror so you can spot any mannerisms you use.

The questions asked come from a survey made on the most common questions asked at graduate interviews. These questions will be asked, with slightly differing wording, in many interviews.

There aren't right or wrong answers to most questions, and how you come across is as important as what you say. Be yourself: if you have to assume a false persona to get the job, it may not be right for you.

Try a practice interview with a friend

Get your friend to ask you the questions on the forms below and to note down how you answer each one. If you have a friend who is also applying for jobs, why not agree to give each other practice interviews? Ask your friend to also assess your non-verbal communication. Having an 'interview buddy' can be a great help in preparing: you can test each other on interview questions, and also share any anxieties or other problems you may have.

You also learn a great deal by being the interviewer. By putting yourself in the interviewer's shoes, you will learn how difficult it is to listen to answers, make notes, encourage the interviewee and think of the next question to ask, all at the same time. This empathy with the interviewer's role will help you to perform better.

Consider putting on your interview suit to get you immersed in the mood and to make it more realistic, and ask for an honest appraisal of how you look.

Interview assessment form

Employers use forms like this to assess interviewees. Get a friend to rate your answers. Score each answer: 1 – fails to meet the criteria, 3 – just meets the criteria, 5 – easily exceeds the criteria.

Question	Criteria	Score
How did you choose your university and why?	Does the person have logical reasons for his or her choice? Did she go through a clear decision-making process, or was it impulsive?	

	Did the applicant research the choices carefully?	
What did you gain from your work experience?	Has the interviewee had much experience?	
	Can he say what has been learned?	
	Can the applicant relate the experience to this job?	
	Did he gain an insight into the business?	
Give an example of when you worked effectively in a team.	Is the example given strong?	
	Did the applicant clearly define her own role?	
	Can she work confidently in a group?	
	Does she establish good relationships?	
	Did she describe the situation, the tasks, her actions and the results?	
Describe a situation where you've led a team.	Is the example strong or weak?	
	Did the interviewee give a well-structured answer?	
	How does he lead? Does he just bark out orders, or can he motivate others?	
What has been your greatest achievement?	What values does she hold: helping others, making money or leadership?	
	Is there evidence of tenacity, resilience, planning or other important qualities?	

What are your weaknesses?	Is he mature enough to admit these? Does he try to improve himself? Are his weaknesses critical to the job?	
Why do you want to enter this career?	Is there evidence of relevant skills? Has she researched the career? Does she show enthusiasm for the job?	
Where do you see yourself in five years' time?	Is his answer realistic? Has he researched career paths? Is there evidence of ambition?	
Who else have you applied to?	Has she applied to similar organizations? Were her applications successful?	
What makes you the best person for the job?	Does she know what her strengths are? How do these relate to the job?	
Have you got any questions?	Are his questions sensible? Do they show evidence of research into the role and organization?	
	Total score out of 55	

Get your friend to rate other aspects of your performance below.
Ignore interview dress if not dressing formally.

	5 = Excellent	1 = Poor	Score (1 to 5) and notes
Appearance	Dressed appropriately/ professionally	Inappropriate dress, untidy	
Posture	Open arms, good posture, leaning forward	Closed/defensive: folded arms slouching, fidgets	
Impact	Smiling, warm, head nodding, confident	Serious, unsmiling, nervous or arrogant. Weak handshake	
Eye contact	Good eye contact	Little eye contact or constantly staring	
Voice	Clear, strong, authoritative	Weak or unclear, too fast or slow	
Attitude	Interested and enthusiastic	Passive, bored, inattentive	
Quality of answers	Articulate: listens carefully; understands questions; builds flowing, well-structured answers	Inarticulate and tongue-tied or rambles on; misunderstands and gives irrelevant answers	
Questions asked	Asks sensible, relevant questions	Few or no questions asked; irrelevant or poorly thought out	
Total Score: 1 to 5 points for each topic. Out of 40			

After your practice interview

Get your interview buddy to mark your performance using the feedback forms above. Ask for encouraging but honest feedback, and ask if you have any particular mannerisms when you're nervous.

If you are giving interview feedback, ask the interviewee first how he or she felt about the performance, before you give your own comments. Feedback should be constructive, factual and specific. For example, don't say, 'You were hopeless!' Say instead, 'Your voice was a little quiet, and I sometimes couldn't hear clearly what you said.'

Were there any questions you had difficulty in answering or thought you could have answered better? Read the tips below and work on your answers before you get a real interview.

The questions with tips on how to answer

How did you choose your university and why?

The interviewer will be looking for logical decision making here. He or she will expect you to have first listed the important factors in your choice: location – not too near or far from home perhaps, campus or city university, grades required, availability of your chosen course, quality of teaching and research. This would suggest a well-organized individual who thinks things through carefully.

They will expect you to have carefully researched the universities which fitted your criteria, before finally visiting them to confirm your choice. Saying, *'Because my best friend went there'* or that your teacher suggested it is not a strong answer – it suggests you are easily led. This is a chance for you to demonstrate your analytical abilities and powers of reasoning.

If you had to go to your local university because of cost, talk about the more general issues you had to think about, such as finance and how you chose your degree subject.

Example answer

I first wrote down the key criteria I was looking for in a university. I was looking for a university with a strong reputation for the subject I wished to study and that was highly ranked in the overall league tables. I also wanted a university in the south of England, but outside London, as London was too expensive, but not too close to where I lived and with a good employment record for its students. This helped me to narrow it down to four possible universities which I then visited. When I visited Kent, I was impressed by the lovely campus and the guarantee of on-campus accommodation for all first-year students and immediately felt at home there.

What did you gain from your work experience?

Most students don't clearly articulate what they have gained from their work experience. They think that employers aren't interested in their 'boring' supermarket or fast-food job, but this is utterly wrong. Your ability to say what you gained from your work experience is more important than the nature of this experience.

One interviewee answered this by telling the interviewer, 'This is personal information I'm not comfortable in sharing.'

Another said, 'You have had two weeks to look at my CV, yet you still need to know about my work experience. This is just typical of HR!'

Employers put great weight on your ability to 'sell' the skills gained in your work experience, to reflect on what you've gained from that experience and to relate these skills to those needed in the job you are applying for. This can be from any type of work, provided you can link the skills you used to those needed in the job. Say that your work in a supermarket required you to work in a busy team, to provide a high quality of customer service, to show flexibility in adapting to a range of different tasks and to deal sensitively with questions and complaints. Anything that demonstrates leadership skills and customer service experience is valuable whether retail, hospitality, call centres – anything that involves putting the customer first. Did you keep your cool when dealing with an awkward customer?

Don't just say the work was routine and boring; instead, find something that you have gained from the experience. Even if you just fried burgers in McDonald's, talk about working under pressure; helping to train new staff; the time-management skills you learned in balancing your work, study and social life; and an insight into how efficiently the business you worked in was run. If you progressed in the job by being given more responsibility or being asked to train new staff, for example, do mention this. Don't criticize any of the companies you've worked for as this suggests you might be a problem employee.

Students who have had part-time jobs have had to learn to manage their time more efficiently and are often more realistic and more mature. They may have learnt that business is about making profits and making sure that tasks get done quickly and well.

If you haven't had much paid experience, mention any voluntary work you've done. Sometimes you may be given more interesting and skilled tasks in voluntary work than in mundane paid jobs. Anything that provides evidence of teamwork, time management, organizing, leading, persuading, taking responsibility or initiative, customer service or working under pressure is worth mentioning.

Example answers

My main student job was at Sainsbury, where I worked on the checkouts during my first two years at university. I was expected to provide a courteous and prompt service and to talk to every customer. Some customers asked me about what I was studying at university and gave me some useful advice on starting a career. Although my work was fairly routine, I built positive relationships with both customers and staff. I enhanced my teamwork skills as well as learning to deal with pressure during busy periods, and I gained an insight into the workings of a large business.

I had a summer job as an assistant at an exam board where I had to work to very tight deadlines and had to rely exclusively on my own initiative. In this fast-paced environment, I had to work competently and calmly under pressure. Assisting a large team of professionals, I developed the ability to prioritize my tasks and to establish and negotiate deadlines. I enjoyed the challenge presented by the responsibility I was given. As my actions had a direct impact upon the team, I developed an ability to learn new skills quickly, to ask for help when unsure and to be diplomatic when liaising between people with conflicting opinions. This also gave me the opportunity to apply my IT skills in a working environment and become increasingly confident in using programs such as Access and Excel.

Give an example of when you worked effectively in a team

This is a classic competency-based question. These are easy to spot, as they nearly always start with *'Give an example ...'* or, *'Describe a situation ...'* of where you used a particular skill. They are best answered by the STAR approach. STAR stands for: **S**ituation, **T**ask, **A**ction and **R**esult. See Chapter 4, 'How to STAR at competency questions', for much more about this.

Firstly you outline the *SITUATION* you were in and also the *TASKS* the team had to complete to achieve its target.

Then talk about the *ACTION* taken by the team. Say what your role in the team was. Describe any problems which arose and how they were tackled. Say what you learned from it. Examples could come from university societies, sports teams, your work experience, group projects on your course – or indeed any situation where you worked in a team; the more recent the example, the better.

Finally talk about the *RESULT* achieved: hopefully, that the team achieved its objectives. Quantitative evidence of a successful result has more impact: *'We were awarded 80 per cent for our group project, the highest mark in the year.'* Or, *'We raised £500 for charity.'* You can talk about a failure if you can draw positives from it. Talk about what you learned from the experience and what you'd do better next time: *'We didn't reach the summit of Mount Everest, but I learned that next time it would be better to take proper climbing boots rather than my old trainers.'* Well, perhaps not quite like this!

One trap that candidates fall into is to fail to mention their own contribution. Their whole answer is based around *'The team did this, we did that'*, but there is no use of the word 'I'. For all the interviewer knows, you might have been doing nothing but sitting around checking Facebook, while the other group members did the work, so do detail your own contribution.

Mention the role you played: leader, ideas person, detail person or harmonizer who keeps the group together. Your role should fit the job you are being interviewed for – if it requires strong leadership skills, give an example where you led the team. Think about the qualities that make you a good team member: your ability to listen, openness, commitment to the team's goals, helpfulness or conscientiousness. A good team player puts the team before his or her own needs.

Example answer

I was a committee member of the university mathematics society, and we decided to help first-year students study for exams by running study workshops. We designed a questionnaire and handed these out after lectures to assess demand, and on analysing the results we found many students wanted the workshops. As students would have a range of queries, we had five final-year students at the workshop, each covering different topics. My role was to book and prepare the venue and advertise it by emailing all first-year mathematics students. We had a large turnout, and the students really liked the idea of having separate advisers for each topic. This also helped with the flow, as nobody was too busy. We also realized that in future we could sell drinks and snacks to raise funds for the society. The event was a big success: we gained a lot of new members and agreed to run more workshops in future.

Exercise: What role do you play in a team?

Role	What you do	What you say
Leader	Directs actions and drives the group forward to get results	*We need to move forward on this.*
Ideas person	Suggests new ways to do things and to solve problems	*Why don't we consider doing it this way instead?*

Motivator	Energizes team when motivation is low through praise, humour, enthusiasm	That's a great idea, Nita.
Evaluator	Logical, objective and offers dispassionate analysis; evaluates competing proposals	Here are the pros and cons of each alternative.
Clarifier	Reflective: summarizes discussions and clarifies objectives	So here's what we've agreed on up to now.
Harmonizer	Maintains harmony; tolerant individuals who resolve differences of opinion and prevent conflict	We haven't heard from Rafa yet. I'd like to hear his views.
Detail person	Memory, timekeeper and spokesperson of the group; records actions and decisions and makes sure they are completed	Are we all in agreement on this?

Write down the roles you favour in group situations.

Add your own if they aren't listed above. Discuss with a friend what roles you take in group situations.

Describe a situation where you have led a team

This is another competency-based question. These are easy to spot, as they nearly always start with 'Give an example ...' or 'Describe a situation ...' where you used a particular skill. It is best answered using the STAR approach described in the answer to the teamwork question above.

Effective leadership involves a complex mix of qualities: a plethora of different skills, such as delegating, motivating, persuading, negotiating, listening, taking responsibility, setting objectives, organizing and adaptability. Good leaders have honesty and integrity, are fair to everyone, trust their team, believe in the abilities of others, encourage initiative, are positive and have drive. It's not surprising that such leaders are hard to find.

Many graduate roles involve the management of staff where you plan and organize the work of your team and also motivate them to complete tasks. The interviewer will be trying to assess your communication skills, what role you take in group situations, your goal orientation and drive.

Before the interview, look through your CV for examples of where you have demonstrated leadership skills. Don't give bland statements such as 'I have a lot of self-confidence and I've always been good at leadership.' If you can't back up such statements with good examples, you are unlikely to get far.

> *A leader is best when people barely know he exists. When his work is done, his aim fulfilled, they will say: we did it ourselves.*
>
> Lao Tzu

Examples you give should describe the team and the task you had. Focus on your own role as leader, on the attributes that led you to take on the role and how these helped you to be successful. If there were any problems, describe how you overcame these and showed evidence of resilience and determination.

A related question is 'What is the difference between a leader and a manager?' Your answer could say that managers organize, plan, project manage and make the best use of the available resources, whereas good leaders motivate and inspire. Different jobs demand different types of leadership. An officer in the armed forces would use an autocratic style of leadership – there isn't time in the heat of battle for a committee meeting! In a consultancy or media organization where many of the staff will have degrees, the leadership style is likely to be more consensual and participative.

> *Management is doing things right; leadership is doing the right things.*

See Chapter 4, 'How to STAR at competency questions', for more help in answering this type of question.

> ### What are the most common questions asked in graduate interviews?
>
> The most common questions asked in a survey of graduate interviews are listed in order below. As you may have noticed, there is a close correlation with the questions asked in this chapter.
> 1. Why do you want this job?
> 2. Have you got any questions?
> 3. Describe a situation in which you led a team.
> 4. Describe a situation where you worked in a team.
> 5. What do you expect to be doing in five years' time?
> 6. What are your weaknesses?
> 7. Who else have you applied to?
> 8. Why did you choose your university, and what factors influenced your choice?
> 9. What are your strengths?
> 10. What has been your greatest achievement?

What has been your greatest achievement?

Don't say that your greatest achievement is getting your degree or going to university, as the interviewer will have heard this a thousand times before. Only use these if you have, for example, had to cope with a disability or study abroad.

You don't have to have won a marathon or swum the English Channel. An excellent choice could be the Duke of Edinburgh's Gold Award expedition, as you have to plan your expedition with your team, decide where you will go, train hard and then complete it over four days. Other possibilities are organizing a musical or fundraising event, getting to grade 8 in a musical instrument, black belt in a martial art or running a half marathon for charity.

Your answer might indicate your values and motivators: helping others, making money or leadership. Show evidence of qualities required in the job, such as resilience, persuading, teamwork, organizing or determination.

Example answer

My greatest achievement was to successfully complete my five-day Duke of Edinburgh Gold expedition in the Pyrenees Mountains. We encountered many problems such as running out of water and having to find an alternative source. We planned our route carefully, so we didn't get lost or have to walk in the dark, as we had a lot of miles to cover each day, but we often had to change our route to an alternative safe path round obstacles. We carried heavy loads, and if someone was struggling, we offered to carry items from his or her backpack and treated minor injuries and blisters. As well as testing my stamina, I learned how to motivate myself and the rest of the team to keep going when the going was tough. I learned that I am a lot stronger and more resilient than I had previously believed.

What are your weaknesses?

A key skill that graduate employers look for is the ability to assess what you are good at and where your weaknesses lie, and then to be able to work at remedying any weaknesses that might affect your performance in the job. This involves being able to self-analyse and to reflect.

Here interviewers are looking for evidence that you are aware of your weaknesses. If you are aware of these, then you can often overcome them or delegate the task to someone who is better at it, so the interviewer is looking for evidence of self-analysis and the ability to introspect.

Interviewers will also look for evidence that you are the sort of person that doesn't rest on your laurels, but instead constantly tries to improve yourself. This is one reason that the question *'What are your weaknesses?'* is so common at interview.

A student, when asked about her weaknesses, thought briefly and then replied: 'Wine, chocolate and men – though not necessarily in that order.' *She got the job!*

Another exclaimed indignantly, 'I didn't think you were allowed to ask that in a job interview!'

Sometimes this question is asked in a different way, such as *'How would your worst enemy describe you?'*, *'What are you bad at?'* or *'What would your best friend say your weaknesses are?'*

Interviewees often choose a strength which is disguised as a weakness, such as *'I'm too much of a perfectionist'*, *'I don't suffer fools gladly'*, or *'I often drive myself too hard'* as they are afraid to disclose their vulnerable aspects. This tactic is used so often that, even if these answers are true, they sound clichéd – the interviewer will have heard it many times. Experienced interviewers will know this trick, and the next question may be something like: *'Okay, you say you are a perfectionist: give me an example of where this got you into trouble.'* If you really are a perfectionist, you should be able to quickly reel off several examples.

Humblebragging

Research at Harvard University[1] found that people who 'humblebrag' were less employable. A humblebrag is a brag disguised as a complaint using self-depreciation. One hundred and twenty-two students were asked to answer the question 'What's your biggest weakness?' Results showed an increased use of humblebragging in job interviews. Students said things such as 'It's hard for me to work on teams because I'm such a perfectionist.' Seventy-seven per cent of the students humblebragged instead of giving a real weakness. Of these 32.8 per cent of the answers focused on perfectionism, 24.6 per cent on working too hard and 14.8 per cent on being too nice. The other 23 per cent who gave honest answers were more likely to be hired.

Don't say that you haven't got any weaknesses as you will be perceived as arrogant or lacking in self-awareness. Everyone has faults, and by being prepared to talk openly about yours, you are showing the interviewer that you are self-reflective. This is a sign of maturity and that you will try to pinpoint and eradicate your weak points. Don't say that your biggest weakness is not being able to answer pointless questions!

The best approach is to describe a weakness you've worked hard to improve and to give examples of what you are doing to exorcise it. Choose a weakness that shows that you are realistic about your capabilities: one that you are already working to correct. Anything that shows that you are a quick learner also helps – this is important to be able to keep up with rapidly changing work environments. A good answer will show that you have identified your weaknesses and have attempted to remedy these. Weaknesses that you've mentioned in your application are obvious ones to choose. For example: *'As you can see from my CV, I didn't perform well in maths at school, as at the time I didn't realize how important it was, but since I went to university, I've realized its importance for many careers, so I made a really big effort in the statistics module in my degree and achieved over 70 per cent.'*

If you have a potential weakness (for example poor exam results), should you mention this at the start or the end of the interview? A study by Jones and Gordon[2] found that interviewees appeared more likeable if weaknesses were disclosed early in the interview and strengths towards the end. Interviewees who disclosed potential problems early on were thought by interviewers to have more integrity and strength of character and thus were not attempting to mislead them. Candidates who mentioned strengths (such as having been awarded a scholarship) later in the interview appeared more modest than those who blurted it out at the first opportunity – these were perceived as boastful.

Why do you want to enter this career?

This is the most common interview question. If you can show that you really are keen to work for the organization, it will reassure the interviewer that you will work with enthusiasm and will be more likely to stay longer with the company. It may be phrased in other ways

Don't answer as one interviewee for a job with a biscuit manufacturer did: 'My lifelong love of chocolate biscuits is the main reason for my interest in the company.'

Or perhaps even worse, the applicant for a finance job, who answered, 'I was closely involved in every aspect of my former company, right up to its bankruptcy.'

such as *'Why do you wish to work for us?'* Mention relevant skills and interests that led you to apply. Interest in the job is an important factor in motivating you, but the interviewer will be looking for evidence that you've analysed your skills and matched these carefully with those required by the organization. You must know a lot about the company, the job and the reason the post is right for you.

Read the employer's website carefully. One employer gave telephone interviews to eight candidates but rejected them all because not one had carefully read the company's website and so couldn't describe the company's products.

> *One interviewee took out his CV and set fire to it to demonstrate his 'burning desire' for the job.*

Don't talk about the salary or perks of the job or give bland answers such as 'It seems a great place to work.' Find some attribute the employer is proud of: their clients, products, individuality, successes, environmental policies or training. With small organizations, you may not be able to do this, but you can still research the industry they are in. For example, if you are applying to a web design company, find out about the latest developments in web design.

This is another chance to put across your unique selling points.

Where do you see yourself in five years' time?

Don't give answers such as *'The world is changing so fast that it's difficult to say what I am likely to be doing all that way ahead.'* This is an opt-out answer: you're not answering the question, and it may suggest a lack of research into the opportunities available.

The interviewer is checking to see that you've carefully researched the career routes open to you within the company and have an idea of the promotion paths open to you. You should try to be reasonably specific – not tying yourself down to a particular route, but showing that you have at least a general idea of where you want to go. The interviewer may also be checking to see if you know about the professional training and any required qualifications for the career. He or she wants to see enthusiasm for the organization and for the challenges and opportunities you would be presented with.

Interviewers are also looking for ambition. If you say that you still expect to be in the same role, you may be marked down as not being ambitious enough, but if you say you expect to be a director, an interviewer may judge that you are out of touch with reality. Talk about how you wish to grow your skills, knowledge and responsibilities over time.

If you are going for a specialist role such as programmer or research scientist, you may wish to enhance your technical skills rather than aiming for management. Many companies now have a career development route for people who wish to stay in the technical side – there is no point in forcing a superb researcher or programmer into a management role he or she doesn't want and isn't suited for.

Example answer

I would hope to grow with the responsibility I am offered and to develop my skills as far as I am able. I would also expect to have completed my professional training successfully, had at least one promotion by this time and be in my first management position. I would expect to be in at least a junior management role within my function by this time.

Who else have you applied to?

Interviewers will expect you to apply to their main competitors, and if you are a strong candidate, they will spend time explaining why you should join them rather than the other companies. They will expect you to have applied to similar jobs in similar companies, so if you have an interview with a bank or retailer, the interviewer will be expecting you to have applied to some of their competitors as well.

One interviewee announced that he would demonstrate loyalty by having the company logo tattooed on his arm.

If you have not, they might doubt whether you're really committed to the career. You should, of course, say that the post you are being interviewed for is your first choice and why. If you haven't yet applied elsewhere, you could say that this is because the present organization is your premier choice. If other firms have rejected you, it's probably best not to mention this.

You may think the interviewer will be flattered if you say that you haven't applied elsewhere, but this won't be the case. The interviewer will assume that you're not sincere or wonder whether your main interest lies in a different career. If you apply to a large number of companies, it may suggest that you lack confidence in your ability to get jobs, and also it will take away from the time available to you for study.

Don't mention applications to unrelated careers

It's wise not to mention applications you are making to different career areas. One student was interviewed for a graduate programme with a top accountancy firm. The interview was going really well, when the interviewer asked which other companies she had applied to. She mentioned that she had applied for a journalism training scheme, whereupon the interviewer asked her how she could reconcile applying for two such different career areas, which she had great difficulty in doing. The interview fell apart from that point on, and she was rejected. She could have made a case for herself by outlining the similarities between journalism and accountancy: both require an inquisitive nature and an ability to ask the right questions; both need good communication skills and an ability to work to deadlines, but her position would have been much easier to defend if she had said she had applied to competitor accountancy firms or related financial jobs such as banking.

What makes you the best person for the job?

The answer to this that most impressed me was that of a *Star Wars* fanatic who answered in perfect Yoda speak. It went something like this:

> 'Why do you think we should appoint you to this post?'
>
> 'Excellent leadership qualities have I. Ready am I to undertake all that of me is required. Within me, strong The Force is. …'

The interview didn't last long.

This is a brilliant opportunity to put across three or four of the key strengths from your unique selling points that make you a bit better than most other candidates. These could be relevant work experience, strong academic performance in subjects related to the work, good evidence for skills that are mentioned in the job description, or evidence of substantial achievements. The term main selling points is better as these points are very rarely unique. Try to back these points up with examples of where you have had to use them. In fact, this is really another way of asking what your strengths are. See Chapter 1, 'Preparing for the interview', for more about USPs.

> *Don't answer like the interviewee who said that she would prefer a job offer from one of the company's competitors, or like another who said,* 'If you don't recruit me, it will prove that your management is incompetent.'

Consider the requirements of the job, and compare these with all your own attributes – your personality, skills, abilities and experience. Where they match, you should consider these to be your major strengths. The employer certainly will. For example, teamwork, interpersonal skills, creative problem solving, dependability, reliability, originality, leadership, and so on, could all be cited as strengths. Where these match up, these are the USPs you will need to talk about. Any evidence of initiative, creativity, solving problems or getting positive results will go down well.

Talk about what you can give to the company rather than what they can do for you. Don't talk about mundane attributes that most other interviewees are likely to have, such as 'I'm a good communicator' or 'I work well in a team'.

Other chances for selling your USPs to the interviewer are when you are asked any of the following:

- What are your strengths?
- Why should we take you rather than the other candidates?
- How would your best friend describe you?

- Tell me about yourself.
- What attributes do you have to make you excel in this role?

Saying, *'I really want this job – all I've read suggests it's an excellent place to work'* puts the emphasis on your needs rather than on what you can offer the organization. Whilst this is acceptable, you are missing a good opportunity to sell the qualities that make you suited to the job.

Saying, *'I am a high achiever who will give you the results you require'* is just hot air unless you can give concrete examples which demonstrate real achievement.

Have you got any questions?

'When is pay day?' might not be the most appropriate question to ask. Questions about salary, holidays, perks and pensions suggest that you are only interested in the job because of the benefits. If the salary hasn't been made clear, it's okay to ask about this, but make sure you have other questions to ask as well.

> *An interviewee asked,* 'When you run background checks on candidates, do arrests come up?'

Good questions are on training and career development. Asking questions allows you to build a rapport with the interviewer. See Chapter 1, 'Preparing for the interview', for a list of questions you could ask.

Finding out more

On the companion website www.palgravecareerskills.com

- Answer tips for many more questions, such as *'What have you gained from your university course?'*

References

1   O Sezer, F Gino and MI Norton, 'Humblebragging: A Distinct – and Ineffective – Self-Presentation Strategy', Harvard Business School Working Paper, No. 15-080, April 2015.
2   EE Jones and EM Gordon, 'Timing of Self-Disclosure and Its Effects on Personal Attraction', *Journal of Personality and Social Psychology,* 24(3), Dec 1972, 358–65.

Index of interview questions with example answers or tips

Index